THE ART OF AMAZEMENT

Rabbi
Alexander Seinfeld

Jeremy P. Tarcher/Penguin
a member of Penguin Group (USA) Inc.
New York

THE
ART OF
AMAZEMENT

·

Judaism's Forgotten Spirituality

JEREMY P. TARCHER/PENGUIN
Published by Penguin Group
Penguin Group (USA) Inc., 375 Hudson Street, New York, New York 10014, USA •
Penguin Group (Canada), 10 Alcorn Avenue, Toronto, Ontario M4V 3B2, Canada (a division
of Pearson Penguin Canada Inc.) • Penguin Books Ltd, 80 Strand, London WC2R 0RL,
England • Penguin Ireland, 25 St Stephen's Green, Dublin 2, Ireland (a division of
Penguin Books Ltd) • Penguin Group (Australia), 250 Camberwell Road, Camberwell, Victoria 3124,
Australia (a division of Pearson Australia Group Pty Ltd) • Penguin Books India Pvt Ltd,
11 Community Centre, Panchsheel Park, New Delhi – 110 017, India • Penguin Group (NZ),
Cnr Airborne and Rosedale Roads, Albany, Auckland 1310, New Zealand (a division of Pearson New
Zealand Ltd) • Penguin Books (South Africa) (Pty) Ltd, 24 Sturdee Avenue, Rosebank,
Johannesburg 2196, South Africa • Penguin Books Ltd, Registered Offices:
80 Strand, London, WC2R 0RL, England

First published by Daas Books in 2002
First Jeremy P. Tarcher/Penguin edition 2005
Copyright © 2002, 2005 by Rabbi Alexander Seinfeld

An application has been submitted to register this book with the Library of Congress.
ISBN 1-58542-418-8

Printed in the United States of America
1 3 5 7 9 10 8 6 4 2

Book design by Jennifer Ann Daddio

While the author has made every effort to provide accurate telephone numbers and Internet addresses at the time of publication, neither the publisher nor the author assumes any responsibility for errors, or for changes that occur after publication. Further, the publisher does not have any control over and does not assume any responsibility for author or third-party Web sites or their content.

Most Tarcher/Penguin books are available at special quantity discounts for bulk purchase for sales promotions, premiums, fund-raising, and educational needs. Special books or book excerpts also can be created to fit specific needs. For details, write Penguin Group (USA) Inc. Special Markets, 375 Hudson Street, New York, NY 10014.

The fairest thing we can experience is the mysterious. It is the fundamental emotion which stands at the cradle of true art and true science. He who knows it not and can no longer wonder, no longer feel amazement, is as good as dead, a snuffed-out candle.

ALBERT EINSTEIN

CONTENTS

FOREWORD

We are here on this earth to grow and, as humans, to grow spiritually. It is therefore necessary for life to provide us with growth opportunities, which take the form of inner challenges. Experiences of loss and failure or, alternatively, of success and opportunity, are thus central to the experience of being human because they provide the defining moments of our lives, when we are handed the opportunity to refine and elevate ourselves spiritually, or not.

Moments of spiritual challenge come to us as tests. They certainly feel that way, but they are tests in the more literal sense as well. In the periods of life when our hearts are not being held to the fire of a test, life gives us the precious opportunity to prepare for those tests. We are wise to seize the opportunity to do spiritual practice whenever we can because, while spiritual testing is an inevitable part of life, the outcome of those trials is never predetermined. Spiritual practice is how you can prepare yourself internally to meet and make the most of life's challenges. Do practice when you are not being tested in order to ready yourself to grow through the testing when it comes your way.

Despite the great service we do to our lives and to the world by practicing spiritually, too often spiritual life is over-shadowed by material concerns. When life is good, we drift away from spiritual practice and so give up the opportunity to bring about the *transformation of self* that a sustained spiritual practice offers. Why is this so?

The answer begins with history. For hundreds of years, autocratic leaders controlled their subjects' spiritual lives to the point that the advent of the Enlightenment was embraced as a time to cast off shackles. Many turned to secular rationalism and never looked back. Unfortunately, there was a baby thrown out with the bathwater.

Over the succeeding centuries, and especially in the last hundred years, the spirituality that lies at the core of our own traditions became so neglected and ultimately invisible that many of us have come to think of spirituality as a feature of Eastern religions but not of Judaism. This is a sad and incorrect distortion of our spiritual way.

In truth, the need for an active spiritual life is universally human, just like art and speech. As Rabbi Seinfeld argues, this essential human function has had nearly four thousand years of development in Jewish tradition. Its masters have created a refined art form. But, like any art form, spirituality needs to speak in the voice and character of the surrounding culture. America has embraced Jewish comedy, music, and food, and it is time that an American-Jewish spirituality be articulated as well.

Perhaps the most important lesson of Rabbi Seinfeld's book is that meaningful spirituality is the vibrant core of all of Judaism. We Jews are fortunate to have a spiritual tradition as old and as rich as that of any culture. Yet for historical reasons, too many of us have been rendered illiterate in basic practices that should be as familiar as Hanukkah and Passover. What Rabbi Seinfeld holds out to you is a Judaism with its spirituality intact. His is a fresh vision that will stir the soul.

This guide to ancient Jewish pathways has the potential to lead anyone toward finding joy and meaning in every aspect of life. The goal, as Rabbi Seinfeld says, is to master spiritual health. When we, as individuals, take steps to increase our spiritual literacy we will also increase our collective spiritual health, and the result we can look forward to is a just, caring, ethical world. That would be a very good station to arrive at, and this book is one of the milestones on that road.

—Dr. Alan Morinis
Author of *Climbing Jacob's Ladder*

Author's Preface

We are witnessing a new stage of human development: a modern spiritual revolution.

As in other historical epochs, the Jewish People have much to offer this tremendous global movement, which is growing slowly but steadily like the dawn.

Yet, paradoxically, Jewish society appears in some ways headed toward darkness—another tragic downturn in a 3,300-year roller-coaster history.

The apparent problem is rooted in widespread ignorance of Jewish thought and custom. Many factors have contributed to this illiteracy, including an alluring scientific-materialist culture (in contrast to an unalluring edifice of meager Jewish ritual); a dogmatic popular stereotype of religion (thanks to nearly two millennia of non-Jewish religious fundamentalism); the Nazi destruction of most of the great Jewish learning centers; and the mere effort of survival. These factors have contributed to the disengagement of half or more of the Jewish People from their rich heritage.[1]

What makes this trend especially troublesome, from even a purely sociological perspective, is that the typical disenchanted Jew has not found satisfying spiritual alternatives. We have scoured the spiritual marketplace and remained unfulfilled. So we halfheartedly uphold a few customs like Hanukkah and Passover, with some vague sense that we (or our children) may one day discover their deeper meaning.

That day has already arrived.

A groundswell of Jews is now discovering Judaism's best-kept secret: there is something going on there. There is untapped wisdom. As many have privately suspected, Judaism is a spiritual gold mine waiting to be discovered. The reader is challenged to make the minimal effort to find one or more nuggets to transform a mundane and material life into a transcendental and spiritual one.

The hardest part of this path, like any journey into unfamiliar waters, is to make the first steps. It would be helpful to have a guidebook to the journey. The present volume is an attempt at such a guide. It outlines the ancient Jewish spiritual arts in clear terms for any spiritual seeker. Each chapter is a stand-alone lesson with step-by-step exercises on how to achieve a particular aspect or level of spiritual awareness. These levels are progressive, so the reader is encouraged to linger at each lesson until completing that set of exercises. Such self-discipline will enable a sincere seeker to use the book as a practical guide to life's subtlest pleasures.

As many of my students know, I often describe Jewish spirituality as meditation, for to live a life of amazement requires a kind of mental discipline and practice that may be called meditative.[2]

However, I moved away from the title *Jewish Meditation* because it did not capture everything that this book sets out to do. The book will indeed speak to those seeking meditation, but also will appeal to those who seek an enhanced spiritual life without getting into meditation.

Many individuals have left their indelible marks here, either directly or indirectly. The full list of acknowledgments can be found at the end of the volume. But the biggest influence on this book has arguably been ancient (and a few modern) texts. The reader will find that the most-cited texts include the written Torah, the Talmud and Midrash, and *Nefesh HaChaim*. The reader may also detect the influence of Rabbi Aryeh Kaplan, whose various works are highly recommended. Please consult the endnotes and the bibliography for more information.

I have constructed the book as a curriculum for anyone—beginner or experienced—to begin transforming our lives individually and collectively. Reflecting this broad audience, the endnotes range from illustrative to technical.

Chapter 1 presents the historical background to this curriculum and to this particular volume. Chapter 2 lays the philosophical groundwork necessary to approach meditative arts adroitly—for the mind should understand and then lead the heart and body. Chapters 2–8 guide the reader progressively through the practices themselves. Chapter 9 unifies the various ideas and practices into a holistic system.

I will consider the book successful to the degree that readers discover a Judaism of profound spirituality, a system that can frame obscure rituals and beliefs with relevance to the twenty-first century. The fortunate few who have already discovered such a perspective may find this book helpful in deepening the meaning of their practice.

Baltimore, Maryland
May 2005

Note on transliterations: as there is no way to please everyone, I have generally followed the Ashkenazi pronunciation of Hebrew, which most authorities agree is preferable for Jews of European heritage. For familiar words I have tried to give both the familiar pronunciation and the Ashkenazi. Readers who are concerned about the appropriate pronunciation of meditations are encouraged to contact one of the resource persons listed in the appendix.

NOTES

1. It is very hard to create an objective statistical description, largely due to competing definitions of who is Jewish and what is called affiliation. The numbers seem to indicate a trend toward secularization. Jim Schwartz, "U.S. Jewish Population Survey," New York: Mandell L. Berman Institute, Graduate School and University Center, City University of New York, 1990, indicates 35 percent of self-reported Jews have no significant Jewish spiritual activity (www.jewish databank.com/njps90/01st.jpg). A more recent survey, Egon Mayer, Barry A. Kosmin, and Ariela Keysar, "American Religious Identification Survey," New York: SUNY Graduate Center, 2001 (www.gc.cuny. edu/studies/religion_identity.htm), suggests this number is now closer to 50 percent. *See also* "2001 Annual Survey of American Jewish

Opinion," New York: American Jewish Committee, 2001. These studies include only self-identified Jews. It may be assumed that many assimilated Jews by birth were not included. *See also* ajc.org/InTheMedia/Publications.asp?did=132&pid=625.

2. The phrase "art of amazement" is not meant to be associated with a similar phrase coined by Abraham Joshua Heschel. Readers familiar with Heschel will notice that the philosophies and pedagogies overlap in meaningful ways yet diverge as well at critical junctures. See Heschel, *God in Search of Man,* p. 43; and *Moral Grandeur,* p. 252.

ONE

•

GETTING STARTED

The Art of What?

•

Breaking Stereotypes

A Brief Historical Background

Key Concepts

Methodology of This Handbook

He who knows it not and can no longer wonder,
no longer feel amazement, is as good
as dead, a snuffed-out candle.

ALBERT EINSTEIN[1]

Try to remember the most spectacular sunset you ever saw.

Picture the setting (likely a beach or a mountaintop): visualize the colors—the oranges and reds, the purples and blues, painted across the sky. How did you feel? Recall the sensation of your mind expanding to the size of the horizon. For at least a moment, perhaps you felt a tremendous joy, calmness, and even a flow of energy. Some have felt a sense of timelessness. Others describe a feeling of awe so overwhelming that one gasps—literally breathtaking.

Take a few moments to recall such an experience, such as watching a sunset, downhill skiing, reaching the summit of a mountain, witnessing a birth, or feeling an earthquake. What these moments all have in common is that, however briefly, you really felt alive! You felt a powerful sense of awe or beauty, bigger than yourself, connected; you felt great! You may have even said, *"Wow!"*

Whenever you find yourself saying *"wow!"* with your entire being then you are probably having a brief transcendental experience.

Unfortunately, although we all relish such profoundly transcendental moments, they occur spontaneously and infrequently, seldom when and where we choose.

The purpose of this book is to help you identify the source of that amazement, to cultivate it, and to experience it daily—even hourly and minute by minute.[2] This practice is the art of amazement.

In course, you will become familiar with several fundamental concepts. These include basic Jewish philosophy—in Douglas Adams's immortal phrase, the "Question of Life, the Universe and Everything"; Kabbalah, what it is and what it does; and Kabbalah's vogue counterpart, Jewish meditation.

BREAKING STEREOTYPES

Popular interest in esoteric Judaism is a recent phenomenon in the secular world.

In modern times, Judaism's scope has been limited for most people to an assortment of traditions, including bar

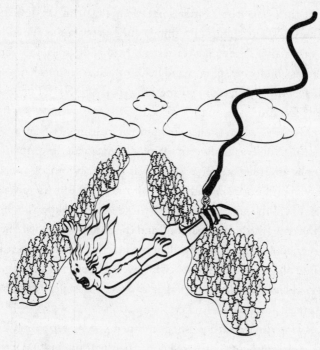

Some people will do almost anything to get their "wow!"

mitzvahs, Hanukkah, Passover, maybe some ancient history flavored with gefilte fish and peppered with a little kvetch.

With similar stereotyping, "meditation" for many conjures up a half-naked Buddha, sitting cross-legged and smiling on the floor.

When Jews do look for spirituality, they often find Buddhism and other non-Jewish systems more alluring than what they had seen in Judaism. Others linger in the Jewish framework, pursuing something called Kabbalah as the key to spirituality. They take classes and read books about upper spheres and lower spheres and fields of wheat, and they usually feel they are learning something special but don't necessarily feel more spiritually satisfied.

My own self-awareness of spiritual yearnings began as a teenager while attending my family's synagogue. Like many people, my religious observance was primarily out of social custom and not penetrated by great meaning. But there was one part of the service that always clicked with me. It was right at the end, before the final song and the announcements. The prayer book called it simply silent meditation, and the organist would play meditative chords while we each selected a passage to read silently. I liked where that took me, to a state of mental calmness. I wanted to go there more often.

Unfortunately, those silent moments were peripheral to the main elements of the religion. The silent meditation was itself at the end of the service, almost an afterthought. There was no guidance and no infrastructure for additional meditative experiences.

In college, I discovered several non-Jewish systems of meditation. Every so often, flyers appeared around campus promoting some visiting holy man's presentation and demonstration of Transcendental Meditation, "yogic flying," and other feats. One of those evenings inspired me to investigate further. I took classes and went on retreats. I read the major books by Indian, Tibetan, and Japanese Buddhists, and I dabbled in the methods. I even had a roommate who would drag me to Hindu religious ceremonies at which henna-decorated people in long robes of white and orange piled fresh garlands on mini idols, sat cross-legged, and chanted in a faraway tongue.

While these enjoyable experiences improved my concentration and planted spiritual seeds, I remained conscious of practicing a distinctive Eastern spirituality—a foreign path, not my own. I felt like an observer, never a full participant. When I met a Japanese Buddhist or an Indian Hindu, I used to think, "Now *there's* a real Buddhist! Now there's a real Hindu!" Even the most secular, assimilated Asian-American from a Buddhist or Hindu family somehow seemed more Buddhist or Hindu than I could ever be.[3]

I know that this feeling of connectedness to *Yiddishkeit* (Judaism) is real and common, because there are numerous popular jokes based on it.

Take the story of the Jewish woman who goes on a difficult journey to visit a famous Indian guru. When she arrives, she is allowed to speak only three words with this holy man who sits in constant meditation. What meaningful three words does she choose to say? "Irving, come home!"

> *Being Jewish is deep karma.*
> ABBOT NORMAN FISCHER (JEWISH BORN)
> SAN FRANCISCO ZEN CENTER[4]

Eventually, I listened to this inner voice and began an investigation into what 3,000 years of Jewish tradition might have to say about spirituality. I was surprised to discover how deeply that tradition was able to speak to me.

I was also surprised to learn I was far from alone. In recent years, many Jews have made the refreshing discovery that they have their own tradition of spiritual awareness and amazement. They discover a Judaism they never knew that is both profoundly intelligent and deeply spiritual, while remaining fundamentally practical.

The Jewish art of amazement is practical and accessible to anyone, regardless of affiliation or personality. It does not demand a radical lifestyle change. On the contrary, the healthy spiritual path requires very small changes in routine while wrestling with larger shifts in perspective. It consists of many interrelated ideas and practices. One must consider, understand, and try each idea and practice on its own merits. It is not an all-or-nothing system.

The system does require thought. Rather than rely on leaps of faith, it is a logical framework. Spiritual fulfillment thereby depends in part on one's intellectual grasp of the philosophical model.[5] To this end, I have divided the book according to logical levels, each one building on the last. A reader who skips ahead will find some concepts unclear. For this reason, it is important to take time to master the first, most philosophical level. Moreover, evaluate your mastery of each chapter before proceeding.

Along this path of personal transformation, there often

runs a subtext of cultural continuity and reconnecting to community. I have met hundreds, or perhaps thousands, of Jews who discovered Jewish spirituality only after having begun their journey elsewhere. Common introductory paths include overtly religious affiliation like Buddhism, Christianity, Hinduism, and Islam, as well as secular pursuits such as academics, the arts, business, journalism, and politics. Many describe their discovery of ancient Jewish spirituality as "coming home."

Interestingly, such people often say that, in retrospect, their life has been a good preparation for entering the Jewish path.

Although this book is primarily addressed to those who are ready to tackle the exercises and grow spiritually, even the casual reader will benefit from processing two important ideas:

- how spirituality and meditation have been integral to Judaism for thousands of years
- how the art of amazement is arguably Judaism's central theme

Some find these two points so compelling that they wonder why they never heard of them before. They wonder how there could be Jewishly active Jews of all stripes who never heard of them. When encountering new and unfamiliar ideas, the reader is encouraged to consult the endnotes for enlargement of the discussion and references.

A BRIEF HISTORICAL BACKGROUND

The very idea of Jewish spirituality astonishes many people, especially Jews. For most of us, Judaism amounts to a set of holidays and rituals like Hanukkah, Passover, bar mitzvahs, and bagels with cream cheese and lox.

Some people are vaguely aware of an esoteric Judaism, associated with certain mysterious texts such as the *Zohar*. Since most of these were first published in the Middle Ages, there is an erroneous popular belief that Jewish mysticism began then.[6]

In reality, meditative disciplines have been part of Judaism since ancient times. Ancient Israel abounded with meditation schools, teachers, and disciples, especially during the First Temple era (ca. 900–500 B.C.E.).[7] These schools were led by spiritual masters known as *nevi'im,* loosely translated as "prophets" but understood more precisely as masters of transcendental meditation.[8]

These masters promulgated many techniques, some of which fit our stereotypes and others that do not. Miscellaneous examples include chanting, gazing at a flame, and breathing techniques. One of the advanced methods involves quietly concentrating on certain letters of the Hebrew alphabet. These meditative practices have survived the millennia, passed discreetly from teacher to student.

In fact, this chain of tradition seems to have originated

well before the First Temple period. For instance, the Bible says of Abraham's son Isaac:

> *Va'yeitsei Yitzhak lasuach ba'sadeh* . . .
> *Isaac went out to* lasuach *in the field.* . . .
> GENESIS 24:63

Biblical commentaries differ widely on the exact meaning of *lasuach*, which appears exclusively here. Some say it involves sitting still, others say it means walking, talking, or even singing. But nearly all commentaries agree that the term is an overt reference to a meditative practice.[9]

The Midrash supports this consensus. *Midrash* means "exposition" and pertains to a compendium of oral traditions that were committed to paper in the form of Biblical commentaries over most of the first millennium C.E. The Midrash contains many details of the stories that are obviously missing from the text of the Torah.[10] For example, the Torah says explicitly that "Terah begat Abraham" (Genesis 7:24), yet never mentions Abraham's mother. Only from Midrash do we know her name to be Amasalai.[11] Thus Midrash, often translated as "legends" or "tales," might be understood as the "footnotes" to the Biblical narrative.[12]

These Biblical footnotes give a context to Isaac's meditation. The Midrash relates that Abraham, Isaac, and Jacob were all steeped in even older wisdom received from Noah's son Shem. Jacob himself spent fourteen years in Shem's academy.[13]

This little-known story indicates the centrality of the contemplative arts to ancient Judaism.[14]

This woven fabric of wisdom and custom sprang from the initiative of one couple, Sarah and Abraham, who died in 1630 and 1592 B.C.E., respectively.[15]

Abraham: Spiritual Giant

In Jewish spirituality, Abraham was the central stalk from which the flower bloomed. He was a spiritual giant whose greatness can hardly be overstated.[16] He independently discovered the art of amazement and its related spiritual principles. He and Sarah became great spiritual leaders. In their prime, they had thousands of disciples (Abraham taught the

And Isaac went out to meditate in the field. . . .

men and Sarah taught the women).[17] They were exceedingly wealthy and opened their tent "on all four sides" to welcome every stranger.[18] The Midrash gives them a very noble image, like unofficial royalty of the Middle East.

It is fascinating to note that Abraham and Sarah lived just before the original Aryans, whose immigration to India in 1500–1000 B.C.E. sparked the beginning of Vedic religion, which later spawned Hinduism, Buddhism, Sikhism, and others. Compare, for instance, the following names:

> *Abraham . . . Brahma*
> *Sarah . . . Sarasvati*

Brahma is the highest god in Vedic mythology and Sarasvati is the primary of Brahma's two wives. In the Torah, Abraham also has two wives, and Sarah is the primary of the two.[19] Does this coincidence point us to the destination of Abraham's children of his old age, whom he "sent eastward, to the land of the East, before he died" (Genesis 25:6)?

From what we know of Abraham's stature as a teacher and leader, it is likely that his progeny became spiritual leaders in their own right. If some of them did reach the Indus valley, it is not hard to imagine them teaching the indigenous population a spiritual system that associates the names of Abraham and Sarah with transcendence itself.[20]

This brief background should intrigue the skeptic and reassure the seeker that Jewish spirituality has the proper credentials to be a true fountain of transcendental wisdom.

KEY CONCEPTS

Seekers of wisdom might well heed the Talmudic counsel: first and foremost, define your terms.[21] Several important terms are used extensively throughout this book, including "Jewish," "meditation," and "spiritual." These words have so many popular connotations as to render them almost meaningless. To achieve clarity therefore requires beginning with precise definitions of terms.

Definitions are debatable. The goal of the present section is for the reader to understand the usage of these terms, not necessarily to accept them.

Jewish

When I ask what *Jewish* means, most people answer vaguely that it refers to what Jews do.[22]

The problem with this definition is that there are many Jews who do many things that one would not call Jewish.

Rather, for the purposes of this book, the term *Jewish* refers to anything taught by the classic Jewish texts, including the Torah (Bible), Midrash, Talmud, Kabbalah, and their classical commentaries. Every concept and practice taught here comes from one or more of these sources.

Spiritual

The word *spiritual* refers to an experience of the soul as opposed to the material experience of the body. Most of our activities have the potential for both material and spiritual experience. The operative difference lies in our awareness, for the seat of spirituality is the mind. Since most of us interact with the world first and foremost with our bodies, our experiences are always going to have a material, or bodily, side; to add the spiritual dimension to an experience, however, requires exercising the mind.

For instance, one can eat ravenously or one can savor food; yet the spiritual act of savoring in no way diminishes bodily fulfillment. Spirituality is very much a state of mind.

Therefore:

- A *spiritual practice* is a regular activity done in order to achieve this state of mind.
- A *spiritual person* is someone with a spiritual practice.

Consequently, both monotheistic prayer and voodoo worship could be spiritual acts. So could creating music, giving charity, or teaching a child to read; even eating, shopping, or playing golf. Conversely, all of these things, including meditation and prayer, could potentially be devoid of spirituality. Spirituality depends on one's state of mind while performing an action, not on the action itself.

This general definition does not mean that all spiritual practices are equally healthy. Spirituality may be compared to food—some types are conducive to good health and some lead to poor health. Similarly, we find that, as with food, the ideal balance of spiritual diet varies from person to person.

However, since the soul does not share the body's physical limitations, it is not possible to overindulge in healthy spirituality.

Meditation

"Meditation" is in everyone's vocabulary, yet it is hard to find two people with the same definition. For many, meditation connotes sitting on the floor, eyes closed, perhaps in silence or perhaps chanting. Some equate it with mental stillness. Others associate the word with relaxation. Still others define it as escapism.

In truth, all of the above may be legitimate meditative practices. The common denominator between them is neither the particular form nor the goal, but the action: Meditation is a practice that involves *focusing the mind*.[23]

Does this definition include reading a newspaper, which involves focusing the mind?

This example clarifies our definition. We do not generally associate reading with meditation because meditation is a *discipline*, a skill that one develops over time. For mastery, mental focus must be practiced on a regular basis, like learning music or sport. Preferably, one should practice daily.

Therefore, newspaper reading might be a meditation, if one were to choose a certain newspaper article and read it over and over.

The untrained mind constantly adjusts and refocuses. Meditation can be defined as the practice of disciplining that natural mental function. Unlike music or athletics, where many of us feel that our physiology prohibits mastery, in meditation the playing field is much more level because success has less to do with physiological factors such as the ear or eye–hand coordination and more to do with willpower.

From a Jewish perspective, it is an interesting fact that the modern Hebrew word for meditation is *meditatsia,* borrowed from English. The authors of modern Hebrew used as much of the classical language as possible, and for modern concepts, such as airplane or psychology, they either invented a new word or borrowed from modern languages, chiefly English. Hence, the Hebrew word for airplane is *aviron,* from the root *avir,* or "air." The Hebrew word for psychology is *p'seekologhia*—adopted from English.

Therefore, since the modern Hebrew word for meditation is *meditatsia,* one might conclude that ancient Israel had no concept of meditation. Why else would the modern Hebraists have had to borrow a word? In fact, the contrary is true. Not only did ancient Judaism include a concept of meditation, it was arguably the core concept of Jewish practice. Paradoxically, the lack of a Hebrew word for meditation actually reflects the centrality of meditative practices to Judaism rather than the lack thereof.

The paradox can be explained by a similar phenomenon in arctic cultures.

In arctic cultures, snow and ice have obvious importance. Consequently, people who live in the arctic have developed rich snow and ice vocabularies. For instance, the following is a list of forty-nine words for snow and ice in the West Greenlandic language:[24]

1. "sea-ice" siku (in plural = drift ice)
2. "pack-ice/large expanses of ice in motion" sikursuit, pl.
3. "new ice" sikuliaq/sikurlaaq (solid ice cover = nutaaq)
4. "thin ice" sikuaq (in plural = thin ice floes)
5. "rotten (melting) ice floe" sikurluk
6. "iceberg" iluliaq (ilulisap itsirnga = part of iceberg below waterline)
7. "(piece of) fresh-water ice" nilak
8. "lumps of ice stranded on the beach" issinnirit, pl.
9. "glacier" (also ice forming on objects) sirmiq (sirmirsuaq = Inland Ice)
10. "snow blown in (e.g., doorway)" sullarniq
11. "rime/hoar-frost" qaqurnak/kanirniq/kaniq
12. "frost (on inner surface of e.g., window)" iluq
13. "icy mist" pujurak/pujuq kanirnartuq
14. "hail" nataqqurnat
15. "snow on ground" aput (aput sisurtuq = avalanche)
16. "slush on ground" aput masannartuq
17. "snow in air/falling" qaniit (qanik = snowflake)
18. "air thick with snow" nittaalaq
19. "hard grains of snow" nittaalaaqqat, pl.

20. "feathery clumps of falling snow" qanipalaat
21. "new fallen snow" apirlaat
22. "snow crust" pukak
23. "snowy weather" qannirsuq/nittaatsuq
24. "snowstorm" pirsuq/pirsirsursuaq
25. "large ice floe" iluitsuq
26. "snowdrift" apusiniq
27. "ice floe" puttaaq
28. "hummocked ice/pressure ridges in pack ice" maniillat/ingunirit, pl.
29. "drifting lump of ice" kassuq (dirty lump of glacier-calved ice = anarluk)
30. "ice-foot (left adhering to shore)" qaannuq
31. "icicle" kusugaq
32. "opening in sea ice" imarnirsaq/ammaniq (open water amidst ice = imaviaq)
33. "lead (navigable fissure) in sea ice" quppaq
34. "rotten snow/slush on sea" qinuq
35. "wet snow falling" imalik
36. "rotten ice with streams forming" aakkarniq
37. "snow patch (on mountain, etc.)" aputitaq
38. "wet snow on top of ice" putsinniq/puvvinniq
39. "smooth stretch of ice" manirak (stretch of snow-free ice = quasaliaq)
40. "lump of old ice frozen into new ice" tuaq
41. "new ice formed in crack in old ice" nutarniq
42. "bits of floating" naggutit, pl.
43. "hard snow" mangiggal/mangikaajaaq

44. "small ice floe (not large enough to stand on)" masaaraq
45. "ice swelling over partially frozen river" siirsinniq
46. "piled-up ice floes frozen together" tiggunnirit
47. "mountain peak sticking up through inland ice" nunataq
48. "calved ice (from end of glacier)" uukkarnit
49. "edge of the (sea) ice" sinaaq

If you examine this list, you may notice the paradox: There are no general words for snow or ice. Presumably, if one were to go to Greenland or Lapland and start speaking about snow in general, one's interlocutor would be puzzled, wondering why you speak so strangely. "What kind of snow do you mean?" they would ask.

We don't find this phenomenon in English, for we seem to have words for *everything*. Yet we do have similarities in the vernacular. For instance, imagine someone were to say, "Today I'm going to do some movements."

Not only would we be puzzled, we would consider such a statement strange. Then the person might explain, "You know—movements: I'm going to put on special shoes and go outside and move my legs fast." Our response would be, "Oh! You're going to go jogging!" In this example, although we have a general word for changing place or position, we nonetheless prefer to speak more specifically.

Jewish meditation is comparable to these examples.

"Meditation" to ancient Jews was like "snow" to Eskimos. The lack of a general word does not indicate the lack of the concept. Rather, there are so many kinds of meditative practices that an ancient Jew would never talk about them in toto. If we were somehow to ask ancient Jews about meditation (using a nonexistent catchall Hebrew word for meditation), they would ask you, "What kind of meditation do you mean?"

Popular meditative arts in classical Judaism run the gamut of forms, including some that resemble our stereotypes of meditation. These include sitting still and focusing on one's breathing, contemplating an object, using a mantra, etc. (Please see table in the Appendix.) The Golden Age of these disciplines was during the First Temple period (circa 900–450 B.C.E.).

Unfortunately, the same social-political decline that led to the destruction of the commonwealth and the exile of most Jews to Babylon paralleled a spiritual decline. Many were misusing these advanced meditative techniques. They sought spiritual shortcuts, which led them away from the central goals of all Jewish practice and toward what in English we call idolatry. Indeed, the Talmud records a tradition that the destruction came primarily as a consequence of widespread idolatry.[25]

Even putting aside these hurdles on the spiritual path, fulfillment did not come easy. The advanced techniques require fluency in classical Hebrew and some actually require one to be physically present in the Land of Israel. By the end of the Babylonian exile, few Jews spoke Hebrew anymore and the Jewish people had been dispersed to many countries.[26]

Consequently, at the close of that historical period, the Jewish leadership (who were both political and spiritual leaders) restricted teaching the more esoteric practices to elite students. For the public domain they developed a large set of basic meditations, by means of which it would be possible for anyone to achieve supreme personal transformation. These basic practices are the basis of this book. They are easy enough to start using immediately in a meaningful way yet profound enough for anyone to enjoy years of spiritual growth.

Kabbalah

Kabbalah is an area of Jewish thought and practice that describes the hidden aspects of reality.

The idea that reality involves more than we perceive with our physical senses is a fundamental Jewish concept. The three non-Kabbalistic textual categories—Torah, Midrash, and Talmud—refer to this concept explicitly. In the Torah, for instance, Moses is rebuffed in his attempt to encounter the Divine "face-to-face":

> *You cannot see my face because no one can see me and live.*
> EXODUS 33:20

The Torah here is telling us that there is more to reality than meets the eye. Kabbalah is a description of the hidden reality and explanation of how the hidden interacts with the observable reality.

This definition will be expanded in Chapter 2.

METHODOLOGY OF THIS HANDBOOK

According to our working definition of "Jewish," Jewish spiritual practices are all ancient. Most were transmitted orally for thousands of years before anyone attempted to describe them in writing. Many remain oral to this day.

As mentioned earlier, these practices vary as widely as the arctic snow. From this vast palette, the present volume will cover only the most basic techniques. I have selected those that, through the test of time, have proven to have the widest application. While stereotypical meditations such as sitting with the eyes closed and focusing on breathing have an important role, they are not for everyone at every time and place. As I will emphasize in later chapters, the art of amazement is ideally not confined to isolated moments, but nurtured at every instant. Rather than dividing our days into the spiritual part and the material part, we strive to combine the two.[27]

The meditations I have chosen cater to that holistic vision. They provide the reader with a "spiritual tool kit" that can enable a new course of enhanced awareness and enjoyment.

Although I have designed the program to be user friendly and self-taught, ideally one would have some guidance or tutoring. To facilitate such relationships, I have added an appendix on worldwide sources of guidance and feedback—individual experts who are available either in person, by telephone, or e-mail to answer questions about any of the topics covered in this book.

Regardless of whether or not one accesses an expert, one can and should seek a learning partner. Learning in pairs has been the Jewish ideal from ancient times. Such a relationship, called a *chevruta* (or *chevrusa*), becomes more than the sum of its parts.[28] As a modern philosopher wrote, "None of us is as smart as all of us."[29] If possible, read this book with a partner; at the very least, discuss it with one. You will gain greater levels of insight than you can by learning alone.

This chapter is called "Getting Started" because it outlines the basic vocabulary necessary to proceed. In order to solidify these terms, please do the following exercises before proceeding:

EXERCISES

1. If you haven't yet done so, mull over these key terms and their definitions until they are clear:

   Jewish . . . Meditation . . . Spiritual . . . Kabbalah

2. What is the relationship between meditation and spirituality?

3. The following terms have not been defined. What do you think they mean?

Amazement . . . Mysticism . . . Transcendental

•

NOTES

1. "The World as I See It," from *The World as I See It.* New York: Philosophical Library, 1949.
2. Cf *Talmud Shavuos* 39b.
3. Psychologists and anthropologists have discovered: *people steeped in their inherited culture tend to be happier than those who encounter cultural discontinuity.*
4. Told to the author by Alan Morinis, author of *Climbing Jacob's Ladder.*
5. Indeed, Buddhism (particularly Theravada) also stresses intellectual understanding in its various meditative curricula. In fact, Walpola Rahula, a Buddhist monk and scholar, argues that "meditation" is a poor translation for the Buddhist term it is supposed to represent, *bhavana,* or "mental development." (He attributes this principle to the Buddha's sermon on mindfulness, "Satipattihana-sutta.") Specifically, Buddhist meditation is "an analytical method based on mindfulness, awareness, vigilance, observation" (p. 66), and the goals include "cultivating such qualities as concentration, awareness, intelligence, will, energy, the analytical faculty, confidence, joy, tranquility, leading finally to the attainment of highest wisdom which sees the nature of things as they are" (p. 118). However, while Jewish meditation demands constant, rigorous intellectual examination, the highest goals are not wisdom or perception per se, rather saintliness and holiness (R. Moshe Chaim Luzatto, *Mesilas Yesharim/Path of the*

Just. New York: Feldheim, 1966). Judaism agrees with Buddhism that mystical truths cannot be empirically verified in the Western sense; however, it is often difficult for a Westerner to commit to a long experimentation period before the subjective verification becomes possible. In contrast, the incremental nature of Jewish meditation lends itself to ready verification.

6. See Bension, Ariel, *The Zohar in Moslem and Christian Spain.* Hermon Press, 1932.

7. Cf I Samuel 19:20–23; there, *Targum Yonasan* interprets NATZAV as MALIF (teaching); see the Radak there. From this passage as well as the Talmud in *Talmud Megilla* 14a and Midrashic sources, scholars infer the widespread, organized study of meditation techniques. Cf Kaplan, *Meditation and the Bible*, p. 152.

8. Not to be confused with "Transcendental Meditation" (with capitals), which is a registered trademark of the Maharishi organization. Cf Rashbam on Genesis 20:7. The root *nun-bet-alef* is based on the two-letter root *nun-bet*, which denotes hollowness or openness; to receive transcendental wisdom, one must make oneself "open."

9. *Talmud Brachos* 26b, *Talmud Pesachim* 88a, *Zohar* 39b, *Bereishis Raba* 60a. Cf the commentary on this verse by R. Baruch Halevy Epstein (1860–1942) in *Torah Temimah* (a commentary on the Torah in many editions by multiple publishers).

10. For the first half of Jewish history, these stories were part of the common knowledge and lore of the people. The progress of time and the forces of history reduced the general awareness of *Midrash* to the point where the information was being forgotten; only then was it set to writing.

11. *Talmud Baba Basra* 91a.

12. Others have compared the relationship between the Torah and Midrash to the relationship between *Cliff's Notes* to *War and Peace* and the actual text. The Torah is the summary version! Rabbi Samson Rafael Hirsch (1810–1887) compared the Torah and Midrash to the notes to a scientific lecture and the lecture itself. Trying to under-

stand the Torah without the Midrash would be like trying to reconstruct a lecture from the notes. The Midrash forms one of three major sections of the Jewish oral tradition. The oral tradition is simply the traditional interpretation of the written Torah. The other two major sections are Mishna (interpretation of Biblical jurisprudence) and Kabbalah (interpretation of Biblical metaphysics).

13. *Talmud Megilla* 16b–17a. According to the chronology of Genesis 11, Shem died when Jacob was fifty; however, Jacob did not leave home to study in Shem's academy until age sixty-three, at which time Shem's grandson Eber had assumed the leadership.

14. Even according to those who regard the Midrash as a subjective Biblical interpretation of rabbis who lived 1,500 years after the forefathers, such stories nonetheless demonstrate that these rabbis viewed their own Judaism profoundly more deeply than as a mere set of rules governing behavior.

15. The customs attributed to Abraham in the Bible seem to be consistent with the archaeological record. See John Bright, *A History of Israel,* pp. 77–79; Joshua M. Grintz, *Uniqueness and Antiquity of the Book of Genesis;* M. Haran, *History of Am Yisroel in the Patriarchal Age; Encyclopedia Judaica,* Vol. 9, pp. 1289–90. See also Lawrence Keleman, *Permission to Receive,* pp. 90–94.

16. See Ramban on Genesis 40:14.

17. *Midrash Bereishis Raba* 39:14, 84:4, *Talmud Sanhedrin* 39b; cf Rashi on Genesis 12:5.

18. *Midrash Bereishis Raba* 48:9.

19. Genesis 23 and 25. Interestingly, Sarah had a handmaid named Hagar; India's ancient Sarasvati river (long ago dried up) had a tributary called Ghaggar or Hakra. See *Rig Veda* 1:13:9.

20. The putative linguistic connections mentioned here form one piece of a growing body of evidence that the major meditative traditions of the East can trace some of their ancient roots to Judaism. This controversial thesis is the topic of current research. For more

information, please contact the author. Cf Barbara A. Holdrege, *Veda and Torah: Transcending the Textuality of Scripture,* Albany: SUNY Press, 1996 (her footnotes are particularly interesting). See also Hananya Goodman, ed., *Between Jerusalem and Benares: Comparative Studies in Judaism and Hinduism,* Albany: SUNY Press, 1994.

21. *Talmud Avos* 6:6.

22. It has been widely claimed that a full third of America's 2.5 million Buddhists are Jewish. (See Rodger Kamenetz, *The Jew in the Lotus,* p. 9. See also the American Religious Identification Survey at http://www.gc.cuny.edu/studies/key_findings.htm.) There are about 5.5 million American Jews and 2.5 million Buddhists. A third of the Buddhists would amount to one in seven American Jews, which seems unlikely. Certainly we would not say that Buddhism is Jewish, even if 100 percent of the Jewish people were practicing it, any more than we would say that breathing is Jewish.

23. Britannica.com defines meditation as a "mental exercise conducive to heightened spiritual awareness."

24. From Michael Fortescue's *West Greenlandic* (Croom Helm, 1984). This word list is probably not comprehensive.

25. Cf *Talmud Sanhedrin* 64a. The Talmud expounds on Nehemia 9:4 as a public acknowledgment that idolatry was the main factor in the destruction. The Talmud then illustrates the Israelites' former zealous idolatry with several anecdotes.

26. *MT Hilchot Tefila* 1:1.

27. Judaism's holism is comparable to Integral Yoga, combining physical, emotional, and mental discipline toward a self-unified approach to transcendence. The difference with yoga is that each of the yogas can stand alone; indeed, most Westerners associate yoga with Hatha Yoga, which uses bodily postures, relaxation etc. to purify body and mind and attain the goal of Yoga, "Self-Realization." According to Judaism, the ultimate goal of transcendence cannot be achieved by one branch of practice alone; rather, must use an integrated approach. Also, yoga emphasizes self-actualization, whereas Judaism emphasizes helping others and transcendence. In

this it most closely resembles Karma Yoga; but has something Karma Yoga does not have, *viz,* the *mitzvos.*

28. The consonant "ch" represents the guttural that sounds like someone clearing their throat.

29. Warren Bennis, *Organizing Genius* (New York: Addison Wesley, 1996), Ch. 1.

TWO

•

THE QUESTION

Of Life, the Universe,
and Everything[1]

•

Big Bang Cosmology

Defining Infinite

Purpose of Life

Purpose of Judaism

The subtlety of nature is greater many times over than the subtlety of the senses and understanding.

FRANCIS BACON[2]

He also put enigma in [human] hearts, such that no one can fully grasp the doings of the Driving Force of Nature.

ECCLESIASTES 3:11

BIG BANG COSMOLOGY

There is an illuminating story about the scientific discovery of the origin of the universe. The story begins in 1915, when Albert Einstein circulated a draft of the theory of general relativity, also known as the theory of gravity. Fatefully, a colleague noticed that these new equations indicated an expanding universe.

Einstein found expansion an unacceptable implication of relativity. After all, astronomers at the time overwhelmingly believed what their eyes saw: that we live in a static universe, infinite in time. Consequently, in order to reconcile his new equations with "objective" reality, Einstein had fudged his equations to avoid the implied expansion.

The following decade, American astronomer Edwin Hubble began to revolutionize astronomy with his unparalleled 100-inch telescope, seeing farther and clearer than anyone had ever seen before. Hubble discovered a sort of Doppler-effect phenomenon called stellar red shift that proved beyond doubt that the universe is expanding. He published his findings in 1929.

That discovery got Einstein's attention. In 1930, the great theorist sailed from Germany to California to see Hubble's evidence firsthand. On the spot, as a sign of his own greatness, Einstein admitted his error.[3] More telling, he later called his fudged equations "the biggest blunder I ever made in my life." That is a heavy statement for anyone to make, but especially coming from the man whom *Time* magazine named the single most important person of the twentieth century. His lapse of rigorous intellectual honesty had led him to miss the historic opportunity in 1915 to reveal mathematically what astronomy would discover fourteen years later.[4]

It is hard to imagine what could have bothered Einstein so much that he fudged the equations rather than accept the revolutionary idea of an expanding universe. The fact that a scientist "cheated" in order to avoid an uncomfortable conclusion is not particularly remarkable. But when that one scientist is considered the greatest since Newton, what bothers him becomes very interesting. Some have suggested that the idea of an expanding universe was just too revolutionary for Einstein to believe. Perhaps; however, his special theory of relativity of 1905 ($e = mc^2$) proved that he was not one to shy away from revolutionary ideas.

If the idea itself did not bother Einstein, we are left with only one alternative source of his malaise: the possible implications of the idea. Which implications? We can speculate simply by considering the idea of an expanding universe. If the universe is expanding, then by mentally "rewinding the tape," so to speak, we arrive at the conclusion that the universe as we know it had a beginning. This theoretical beginning is known today as the big bang.

Today, most people accept the big bang idea. This widespread acceptance is remarkable on two counts: it is a very recent theory, still under intense scrutiny and revision; moreover, it completely reversed the scientific worldview on the nature of nature. Scientists themselves more than others regard the big bang a remarkable paradigm shift. Consider the observation of Stephen Hawking, another of the twentieth century's great physicists, who called the discovery of an expanding universe a "great intellectual revolution of the twentieth century."[5]

Why does the origin of the universe matter? It may be an

interesting theoretical problem, but does it really qualify as a "revolution"? The atomic theory was a great revolution because it teaches that 99.9 percent of matter—the stuff all around us—is empty space and it paved the way for countless technological innovations. The special theory of relativity led to atomic energy and weapons. Keynesian economics revolutionized the way in which we regulate markets and banks. Psychotherapy has impacted millions of lives. But how has the big bang theory affected us personally?

Perhaps the most relevant consequence of the big bang theory is what it implies. Maybe the implications are so enormous that even Einstein didn't want to face them. Whether his reaction was conscious or primarily subconscious, we do not know. But we do know that when he fudged the equations and delayed the big bang theory by a decade, he also delayed our confrontation with all that that theory implied.

Now, it seems reasonable to assume that no implication should have bothered Einstein the man of science, but that one particular consequence of the big bang theory may have indeed made Einstein the Jew or Einstein the human uncomfortable. For if the universe as we know it indeed had a beginning, any thinking person must ask: *What came before that?*

It is an unavoidable question. By definition, however, science cannot answer it, for science deals only with what can be observed and/or measured.[6]

DEFINING INFINITE

Where science does not tread, Judaism does. Judaism agrees that the universe has existed for a finite period of time. Indeed, Judaism has always held that the universe had a beginning, and one early source describes a universe that is billions of years old.[7]

Our sages, from Abraham until the present, have contemplated the mystery of what came before the universe. They answer that before the big bang something does in fact exist. This something is nearly incomprehensible and the sages found only one affirmative description for it in our language—that, unlike existence within the universe, that which existed prior to the big bang is completely without boundaries or borders in any dimension.

For want of a better word we call this "thing" *infinite*—or *The Infinite*, since, as will become clear, there can be only one such entity.

It is important not to confuse this term with mathematical *infinity*. Mathematical infinity can have parts. The Jewish concept of Infinite completely lacks external or internal boundaries.

It is also important not to think of the Infinite as an anthropomorphic being or god. Scrap all concepts of "God" that you acquired growing up in a Westernized world. There has been no greater setback for transcendental philosophy and theology than Michelangelo's depiction of God as an old man with a long, white beard. That which is infinite is something beyond the ability of our minds or language to name or define. Our mystics have compared the effort to someone attempting to grasp sounds with his hand. A hand and a sound are simply not compatible.

Even the word *infinite* is a limiting name, because, like all names, it excludes other possibilities. By definition, the Infinite must include all possibilities. But we have no better word than "infinite" to describe that which goes on forever. It seems that, for finite creatures like us, an effort to imagine infinity is no more plausible than my desktop computer appreciating these words as I type them. We're simply not built for that.

Yet we can perhaps get a shadowy glimpse of infinity through analogy.

We live on the surface of what seems to be a small planet.

Or is it so small?

Imagine that the Earth were the size of a basketball. The biozone, the region that supports all of life on the Earth, would be the thickness of a sheet of paper. In other words, from our vantage point, the Earth is actually immense! It is so large that the mind has difficulty grasping its size. Our familiarity with globes and other maps has tricked us into reducing the Earth in our mind's eye, when in fact it is enormous.

Yet the Earth is minuscule in comparison to the sun— the volume of the sun is 1,000,000 times that of the Earth!

Of course, our sun is a star. Try stargazing on a moonless

night. With a clear sky (and especially in winter), the whole of our galaxy sprawls brilliantly across the nighttime sky. It is a gorgeous spectacle to behold. Now, when gazing at our average-sized galaxy, the Milky Way, remember that our sun is a smaller-than-average star, located near the outer edge of the galaxy. The Milky Way has some 100,000,000,000 stars (10^{11}), most of which are larger than our sun.[8]

But many of what appear to be stars in the sky are actually themselves galaxies full of *billions of stars*. How many such galaxies are there? As many as 100,000,000,000 (10^{11}).

When we multiply the number of galaxies time the number of stars in a galaxy, we arrive at the current estimate for the number of stars in the known universe: 10^{22} (in long form, that is 10,000,000,000,000,000,000,000). Note that this estimate refers only to the visible universe—who can imagine how far it stretches beyond that?

How do we make sense of a number like 10^{22}? Such a number is, for all practical purposes, absolutely meaningless. Nobody has a grasp of that many stars.

One approach to making sense of it is to compare this number to other large estimates. For instance, estimates for the number of grains of sand on the world's beaches range from 10^{13} to 10^{20}. *This means that there are more stars in the universe than there are grains of sand on all the beaches on Earth.*[9] How many more? Not just a few—anywhere from one thousand times more to a billion times more!

That's not just big. That's huge, unimaginably vast— immense. When confronting such a scale, our language falters.

And we should not forget that the stars themselves are separated by vast expanses of empty space.

Yet we have not even come close to grasping infinity. As unbelievably vast as this universe is, we haven't even begun to scratch the surface of imagining something infinite.

Even more wondrous than that vastness before us is the fact that we are here to contemplate it. Here we are on our lonely little planet, the third stone from a small sun in one corner of one of these billions of galaxies.

Of course, our planet is unlike every other stone we know in the cosmos. It is a climate-controlled spaceship, racing through the vacuum of space at thousands of miles per hour. If the Earth were slightly closer or farther from the sun, humans could not live here—we would either freeze or burn. Yet we not only live; as a species, we live well. Consider some of our planet's many extraordinary features:

- Perfect chemical elements for life
- Abundant natural resources
- A convenient blanket of air to breathe and to keep our temperatures mild
- An ozone layer in the atmosphere to keep out cosmic radiation
- A particular geological history that favored human life
- Minimal killer comets and asteroids due to influence of Jupiter

- Right distance from center of galaxy for heavy
  elements but minimal cosmic radiation
- Perfect orbit to keep water liquid
- Large moon at right distance to stabilize tilt

Could another delicate planet like ours exist in the universe, or are we alone? Indeed, the cosmos are unimaginably enormous. Yet, despite this vastness, the Earth's extraordinary features have led some scientists to conclude that Carl Sagan probably overestimated the number of alien civilizations out there. According to conservative scientific estimates, it is unlikely that *any* other planet with complex life exists in the universe.[10]

> *Almost all environments in the universe are terrible for life. It's only*
> *"Garden of Eden" places like Earth where it can exist.*
> DONALD C. BROWNLEE, ASTRONOMER
> CHIEF SCIENTIST, NASA'S STARDUST[11]

From that perspective, stargazing becomes an awesome, speechless experience.

Most people have gone stargazing at one time or another. The stars are clearest and most beautiful when viewed far away from city lights. Recall a time when you saw them under such ideal conditions. They were surely very beautiful. And when one stares at them long enough one starts to wonder, *How far does it go?* Well, of course it goes on forever.

But how could it go forever? There must be an end. *But if there is an end, what's beyond that?* Must be more stars. *But how far do they go?*

Pretty soon you are either fast asleep or totally confused. But this is a wonderful exercise in trying to grapple with infinity.

> *The odds against a universe like ours emerging out of something like*
> *the big bang are enormous. . . . I think clearly there are religious*
> *implications whenever you start to discuss the origins of the universe.*
> *There must be religious overtones. But I think most scientists*
> *prefer to shy away from the religious side of it.*
> STEPHEN HAWKING[12]

Even the greatest imagination falls short because it identifies infinity with bigness. It is true: by the Jewish definition, the Infinite is infinitely big; or, more accurately, beyond any measure of bigness. But it is also infinitely small—that is, inscrutably precise beyond any measure of smallness. Within a cubic inch of matter there are approximately 10^{21} atoms, which is the same number as stars in the universe! Unimaginably tiny, and we can now measure with precision the size of atoms! *And the Infinite—by definition—is immeasurably more precise.* Too, by definition, the Infinite must also be infinitely beautiful. And frightening. And wise. This Infinity seems infinitely less comprehensible than the linear mathematical definition. How can we grasp it?

Really, we cannot grasp it. We have to resort to metaphor, and our word "infinity" is the best we have. The word *infinite* means "without end." A finite thing has borders, boundaries. Matter is finite. Energy is finite. Time is finite. Our thoughts are finite. Infinity, in contrast, has no ends, borders or boundaries. It goes on forever in every direction in every dimension.

An infinite entity never stops, neither at the planet Earth nor at a human being. By definition, then, this Infinite is everything. It is also everywhere. And all the time. (*More accurately: timeless.*)

Think about what those words imply: *everything, everywhere, all the time.*

The words imply, among other things, that everything we perceive in this world is "part" of the Infinite, even though the Infinite as defined above cannot have parts.[13]

Herein lies a fundamental paradox. How can the universe exist separately from the infinite? How can the two coexist? For if the infinite is truly infinite, then there should be no finite. Yet we know there is a finite, so how can there be an infinite? How do we conceptualize the relationship between the two?

This fundamental question leads to the second fundamental principle of Jewish philosophy. The first principle is that there is an Infinite that is infinite in every possible way and therefore not bound as we are by space and time.

The second principle can be illustrated with the following metaphor: Imagine yourself at a costume party. Everyone is dressed up; there are clowns, gorillas, one or two George Bushes, and so on. Now, imagine one of the gorillas approaches you and says, "Guess who?"

Your response is going to be to look at his height and try to guess: "Dave!"

"No."

You examine his build more carefully, and guess again: "Joel!"

"Nope."

You analyze his voice and guess again: "Mike!"

"You got it!"

Now, what is Mike going to do after you guess correctly? Of course, he will take off the mask.

The mystics explain that this universe is a mask for the Infinite, a finite facade masking its true infinite nature. For those who pursue Jewish spiritual practices long enough to recognize the reality behind the mask, for them the mask is removed.[14]

> *If the doors of perception were cleansed everything would*
> *appear to man as it is, infinite.*
>
> WILLIAM BLAKE

EXERCISES

1. Meditative posture and contemplating eternity
   This exercise works best if you have someone read the following
   three paragraphs aloud while you follow the instructions.

To prepare for meditation, sit in a comfortable chair (or on the floor, if more comfortable), with the back straight and shoulders relaxed. Close your eyes and let your breathing become steady. Lift your right foot and rotate it three times. Repeat with your left foot. Lift your right hand and make a fist for three seconds. Repeat with your left hand. Rotate your right shoulder three times, then your left. Finally, stretch your head to each side for three seconds, then downward. Keeping your eyes closed, you are now in a basic meditative state.

Contemplate eternity: While keeping the eyes closed, try the following visualization technique taught by Rabbi Eliyahu Dessler:

Imagine the ocean, and the beach, and on the beach there is an enormous pile of sand—the highest in the world. It comes to a perfect point at the top. There is no wind, no noise. Suddenly, from over the ocean, a great bird arrives, flies up to the top of this enormous pile of sand, picks up one grain of sand in its beak, and flies back over the ocean. Then a thousand years pass, when nothing happens; no wind, no rain, the pile of sand remains as it is. Then, after a thousand years, another enormous bird arrives from over the ocean, flies to the top of this enormous pile of sand, removes one grain and returns to whence it came. Another thousand years pass when nothing happens to the pile of sand. Then, after a thousand more years, another bird arrives from over the ocean, flies up, removes a single grain of sand, and flies back over the ocean. How many thousands of years will pass before there will be a noticeable dent in the pile of sand? And how many eons upon eons will pass before the pile of sand is reduced to nothing? When you begin to imagine this vast, vast expanse of time, *you haven't even begun to scratch the surface* of eternity.[15]

2. Contemplate the infinite-finite relationship

Metaphorically, the infinite may be compared to light. When passed through a prism, white light separates into seven colors. These distinct colors represent the physical, finite universe. However, there is only one source of light and only one essential light. What we perceive is the result of a filtering process.

Picture the prism in your mind's eye. Contemplate the symbolism for the natural and the Infinite.

•

Why Create the Universe?

Due to the insurmountable barrier between our finite minds and the Infinite, we can never know about what we would call a motive for the creation of the universe, and if there was a motive, we have no basis for understanding what that motive might have been. For our concept of motive implies something needed, hence lacking; yet by our current definition, something infinite does not lack.[16]

Rather, instead of discussing motive, Jewish philosophy addresses this question in terms of the universe's function.

First, our definition of *infinite* needs fine-tuning. It is not precise to say that the Infinite lacks nothing. In fact, there is one thing that, by definition, the Infinite does lack: *finiteness.* In other words, by saying that the Infinite has no lack—we acknowledge that it lacks lack!

But how can something simultaneously lack and not lack?

Consider the same concept via a different description:

According to Jewish tradition, the Infinite, being infinite, includes in its essence every possible nuance of what we call goodness. One such attribute is the quality of giving. But, by definition, giving requires both a giver and a receiver. How can the Infinite express or actualize the quality of giving? Who or what is there to give to, when the Infinite by definition is everything, everywhere, all the time?

The only possibility of infinite giving is for the Infinite to create receiver "within" its infiniteness, as it were. In order to do so, the Infinite needs to "contract" some of its infiniteness to make "room" for the finite universe. Kabbalah calls this phenomenon *tsimtsum,* which some interpret as "covering" its infinite essence since by definition it cannot become any less infinite.[17] Since we are finite we cannot fully grasp this process and any description of it is going to fall short. But that essential infinite quality of giving is, according to Judaism, the purpose of the big bang and of our existence on this planet. The big bang is (or was, from our time-bound perspective) the ultimate expression of giving. This world is the Infinite's gift to itself (so to speak)—it created a lack in order to fill the lack![18]

This model resolves the paradox—not how, but why something would simultaneously lack and not lack. The answer is: in order to give. Infinite altruism. Contrast this description with a human altruist: People who give do so because in that particular situation it feels better to give than not to give. In contrast, an Infinite altruist gives with absolutely no possibility of receiving anything in return.

Incidentally, we have received from the ancients a detailed description and explanation of how an Infinite creator and a finite creation coexist and interact. This tradition is called "Kabbalah," the chief work of which is the *Zohar/Book of Splendor*. For the average person to open the *Zohar* and start reading would be analogous to a person who doesn't know arithmetic to read a treatise on quantum mechanics. The wisdom is potentially available to all, but there are prerequisite steps to take. To master the art of amazement is to learn the arithmetic of Kabbalah.

PURPOSE OF LIFE

It should now be clear that every particle in the universe, including ourselves who are the most complex arrangements of particles in the universe, has a definite purpose. Our purpose, quite simply, is to receive—to receive goodness or happiness. To receive pleasure.[19]

Herein lies Abraham's great, historic insight. The Midrash tells us that as a child, Abraham looked around and saw a magnificent, intricate world. Where did it come from? he wondered. Nothing comes from nothing, and surely nothing so beautiful and complex, he reasoned. He considered some of the dominant beliefs in Mesopotamian society, that the heavenly bodies are the source of existence. But, he objected, if the world came from something finite, where did that come from? Somewhere back in the chain of cause and effect there must have been something infinite that started it all!

The idea of an unmoved mover that caused the universe was not itself an unparalleled intellectual leap. Others have reached the same conclusion. The Torah itself mentions several such people who predate Abraham.[20]

Abraham's innovation was to carry the logic a step further: If the creator is indeed infinite, then by definition it must not lack anything. Infinite, after all, means that it has no limits, no lack. But if it has no lack, it could not have created this universe for itself. Therefore, he concluded, it must have created this universe for us! For our benefit, for our pleasure!

Hence, with a profound grasp of human purpose, Abraham resolved to seek all of life's pleasures, both the material and the spiritual. He recognized that there is actually a hierarchy of pleasures and that the higher pleasures can offset the lower ones. He and Sarah developed wisdom on how to attain the highest, namely spiritual, pleasures. They transmitted this wisdom to their children and grandchildren and the bulk of it survives until today in the various texts collectively called Torah (see Chapter 1).

PURPOSE OF JUDAISM

Abraham's goal—the pursuit of pleasure or happiness—remains the essence of Judaism. This idea comes as a surprise to many people, and is easily misunderstood. There are two common misconceptions: that spirituality is concerned only with higher-order experiences of the intellect and emotions; and that pleasure means hedonism.

Rather, this philosophy does include physical pleasures: that is, any experience that a person enjoys with one of their five senses. Either you smell it, touch it, taste it, see it, or hear it. Judaism views physical pleasure as central to living a good life. The Infinite made a physical world not to frustrate us, but for us to enjoy.

In fact, the tradition considers it a moral obligation to enjoy life's physical pleasures. For instance, consider the very first mitzvah of the Torah. While we have yet to define mitzvah, it may be loosely understood as a precept. What is the Torah's first mitzvah? It is not "Be fruitful and multiply." Nor is it "Do not eat from the tree of knowledge." In fact, upon a close reading, the text plainly states that the very first mitzvah is "From every tree of the garden you must eat" (Genesis 2:16).[21]

Judaism is first and foremost a system of enjoyment—qualified and disciplined perhaps, but real enjoyment nonetheless. Therefore, for example, Judaism considers it a mistake to refuse an opportunity to taste a new kind of fruit.[22]

The concept may be compared to being served dinner at home: When your parent, spouse, or roommate prepares a new, exotic food, you may very well wish to pass but refusing at least to try it will surely be harmful to the relationship.

EXERCISE

Are you a total connoisseur of aesthetic pleasure?
Use your senses: notice colors, smells, and shapes.
Appreciate the details of the world around you. Start
a journal of your senses and keep a record of what

new things you notice. Note five new points of awareness every day for thirty days.

•

Yet, one should avoid equating pleasure with hedonism. Pleasure refers to all kinds of pleasures, detailed in the next chapter. We have the ability to derive pleasure from everything we experience in this life: every pencil, every penny, every gum wrapper, every computer, every flower, every person, every moral dilemma, and every project.

Take the time to review these ideas until they are clear. The majority of this book deals with the practical application of this philosophical foundation. Therefore, because it is important to have a solid theoretical foundation, it may be beneficial—perhaps even necessary—to return occasionally to this chapter for review.

In the words of Dr. Gerald Schroeder, a nuclear physicist who has explored the intersection of science and spirituality, once we grasp the concept of a transcendental Infinite that created and sustains this mask we call the universe, we can take the next step:

> [We can then] investigate how we might capture the all-too-rare rush of joy sensed when we chance upon the transcendent. Instead of waiting passively for it to happen, imagine being able to have that joy a permanent partner in life. That would be called getting the most out of life.[23]

To take this next step, to begin to grapple with the Infinite, is the historical essence of being a Jew, or more precisely, a *Yisrael* (Israel). *Yisrael* means "one who grapples with the Infinite." The first time that the word appears in the Torah is at the conclusion of Jacob's all-night wrestling match with an angel. The match is a draw and before the angel leaves, he says, "Your name is now Yisrael, because you've wrestled with the Infinite and you've done pretty well."

The metaphor is clear: *B'nai Yisrael*—the children of Israel—are the heirs to Jacob's struggle. We do not relate to the struggle as a literal wrestling contest, rather as a mental and emotional search for the ultimate wisdom and experience.[24]

EXERCISES

1. Based on this chapter, *what is Judaism?*

_____

_____

_____

_____

2. Before you proceed, reread this chapter as many
   times until you fully grasp the concepts. It is
   tempting to proceed before struggling to achieve
   total clarity. However, subsequent chapters depend
   largely on absorbing the first ones.

Make your ears attentive to wisdom, incline
*   your heart to understanding;*
only if you call to understanding and give your voice
*   to discernment . . .*
if you seek it like silver, and like treasure search it out,
then you will understand awe of the Infinite and
*   knowledge of its manifestation you'll find.*

SOLOMON, PROVERBS 2:2–5

•

NOTES

1. The phrase "The question of life, the universe and everything" is a
   creation of Douglas Adams in his book series, *The Hitchhiker's Guide to
   the Galaxy,* and its use as a chapter title here is not meant in any way
   to disparage this fine literary work.
2. Bacon, Francis, *The New Organon and Related Writings,* p. 41.
3. Christianson, *Edwin Hubble: Mariner of the Nebulae,* p. 210.
4. Gamow, George, *My World Line,* p. 150. Cf John Gribbin, *In Search of the
   Big Bang,* p. 91; also Timothy Ferris, *Coming of Age in the Milky Way,* p. 205.
   Although the big bang model was challenged throughout the twentieth century, several astronomical observations supported the the-

ory, such as the discovery of cosmic background radiation in 1965. In the late 1990s astronomers made observations of type IA supernovae that could not be explained by other models (cf Yarris 1999).

5. Hawking, *A Brief History of Time,* p. 39.

6. According to Sir Martin Rees, Astronomer Royal of the U.K. and former director of the Cambridge University Institute of Astronomy, the physics of even the moments *after* the big bang is "speculative" (*Before the Beginning,* p. 160). Even superstring theory only attempts to explain the process of creation ex nihilo, not the ultimate cause.

7. Rav Yitchak of Acre (thirteenth century) states: "I, the insignificant Yitzchak of Acre, have seen fit to write a great mystery that should be kept very well hidden. One of God's days is a thousand years, as it says, 'For a thousand years in Your eyes are as a day . . .' (Psalms 90:4). Since one of our years is 365¼ days, a year on high is 365,250 of our years. . . . This is to refute those who believe the duration of the world is only 49,000 years, which is seven Jubilees [because 365,250 x 5,000 'years' since creation = 1.8 billion years]" (*Otzar Hachaim,* pp. 86b–87b). For a brief but cogent scholarly treatment of this and other sources, please see Ari Kahn, *Explorations,* pp. 285–295.

8. Estimates range from 100 to 500 billion. Cf Dr. Sten Odenwald, *Ask the Space Scientist,* "Exactly How Many Stars Are in the Milky Way?" at http://www.astronomycafe.net/qadir/q76.html. See also "How many visible stars can you see from the Earth?" (http://www.astronomycafe.net/qadir/q81.html) and *ibid.*/q1118.html.

9. A number of estimates of grains of sand on the planet can be found on the Internet, ranging from 10^{13}–10^{21}. The University of Hawaii Department of Mathematics arrived at the figure of 7.5×10^{18}. Their calculations are available online at http://www2.hawaii.edu/suremath/jsand.html.

10. Ward, Peter, and Donald Brownlee, *Rare Earth* (Copernicus Books, 2003). The authors argue that complex organic life is unlikely to

have developed anywhere else. Their thesis does not address the speculation that non-carbon-based life may exist elsewhere.

11. Quoted in "Maybe We *Are* Alone in the Universe, After All," *New York Times*, Feb. 8, 2000, p. D1.

12. John Boslough, *Steven Hawkings' Universe,* p. 121. Cf Dr. Sten Odenwald's answer to the question, "How can an infinite universe have a beginning in time?" in *Archive of NASA IMAGE Space Science Questions and Answers* (/a11839.html).

13. Rabbi Bachya explains this paradox: "These three attributes are one in meaning and we should see them as one. They do not imply any change in the Infinite's profound essence, and neither the postulate of randomness nor plurality of its essence, because what we should understand by them is that the Infinite is neither nonexistent, nor created, nor plural. If we could express the concept of the Infinite with a single word that would in one stroke include these attributes as reason comprehends them, so that these three attributes would come to mind with the use of the one word just as they do when we use the three words, we would employ that word to express the concept. But since we do not find in our spoken languages a word that would indicate the true concept of the Infinite, we express the concept with more than one word" (*Chovot ha-Levavot,* Vol. I, I:10, my translation). Bachya also cites Aristotle: "Negatives give a truer conception of the Infinite's attributes than affirmatives" (*ibid.*) Alshich (*ha-Kadosh*) seems to learn Deuteronomy 32:9 *"Ki chelek Hashemimo"* as a reference to the manifestation of an Infinite essence into many finite expressions. See Alshich on *Exodus* 1:1, available in English: Alshich, Rabbi Moshe, *Midrash of Rabbi Moshe Alshich on the Torah.* Trans. Eliyahu Munk (New York: Lamda, 2000), p. 339.

14. Dessler, *Strive For Truth (Michtav Me-Eliyahu).* Trans. Aryeh Carmell. New York: Feldheim, 1978, Vol. II, pp. 236–251; Tatz, *World Mask* (Southfield, Mich.: Targum Press, 1995), Ch. 2–3. Compare this traditional teaching with modern cosmology: "The physical world can be for all measurable intents and purposes infinite, but this infinity is hidden from us as thoroughly as though it were stuffed

inside a black hole." (Dr. Sten Odenwald, *Ask the Astronomer* Web site, http://www. astronomycafe.net/qadir/ask/a11404.html)

15. Adapted from Dessler (*op. cit.*), Vol. 1, p. 34.

16. *American Heritage Dictionary* defines *motive* as "an emotion, desire, physiological need, or similar impulse acting as an incitement to action."

17. See R. Shneur Zalman Liadi, *Likutei Amarim Tanya*, "Shaar Hayichud," Ch. 5–7. His discussion is based largely on the Ari's (R. Chaim Luria, *Kitvei Ari*) interpretation of the first chapter of R. Shimon bar Yochai, *Zohar/Book of Splendor*.

18. This is a basic understanding of "He created the world only for His glory" (*Talmud Avos* 6:11).

19. Luzatto, Rabbi Moshe Chayim, *Daas Tvunos/The Knowing Heart: The Philosophy of God's Oneness*, Feldheim, 1982, p. 17; Luzatto, *Mesilas Yesharim/Path of the Just*, Feldheim, 1966, p. 17.

20. Such as Noah and his children.

21. This interpretation is a departure from Rashi but is supported on several accounts: the doubled-verb "eating you shall eat," which indicates an intensity often translated as "surely"; the position of the verb "commanded" before the positive and the negative command's position in the subsequent verse, as well as the sources cited in footnote 19. See Gra in *Ederes Eliyahu*, Rabbinu Bachaya; Finkel, R. Nosson Tzvi, *Ohr Hatzofon* 1:2; and *Meshech Chachma*.

22. *Y. Kiddushin* 4:12, at the end. Cf *MB* 225:19. Compare the Mishna in *Talmud Sanhedrin* 37a: *kol echad v'echad chyav lomar, bishvili nivra ha-olam* ("Each and every person must say, The world was created for me"). See also the famous statement of Rabbi Eliezer Hakaper in *Talmud Nazir* 19a (and elsewhere).

23. Schroeder, Gerald, *The Science of God*, p. 89. *Compare:* "Seek the Infinite, for that alone is Joy unlimited, imperishable, unfailing, self-sustaining, unconditioned, timeless. When you have this joy, human life becomes a paradise; the light, the grace, the power, the perfection of that which is highest in your inner consciousness, appear in your everyday life" (Swami Omkarananda, attributed).

24. Cf *Targum Onkelos* to *Genesis* 32:29 (see Bibliography for details).

THREE

·

PLEASURE

The Art of Amazement

·

Body, Soul, and Amazement

The Pleasure Wave

Mind Control and Meditation

Prophecy: Ultimate Amazement

The most incomprehensible thing about the universe
is that it is comprehensible.
ALBERT EINSTEIN[1]

The previous chapter defined the wonderful purpose of human life: to receive goodness and pleasure. Judaism is a system for cultivating pleasure.

Some find this perspective astonishing and they react in one of two ways.

Some are highly receptive—"It sounds too good to be true, but if that's what life is for, who am I to argue?"

Others are skeptical—"If it is true, why is there suffering in the world?"

These two reactions are examples of the cliché about a glass being half empty or half full. One can choose to see life as essentially painful (with some pleasure mixed in) or essentially pleasurable (with some pain mixed in).

We can spend years learning
how to create wealth, but rarely
consider how to enjoy it.

Both the optimist and the pessimist have the ability to receive and to cultivate the pleasures offered us. The only prerequisite is the wisdom to discern real pleasure and to cultivate it.

Unfortunately, our schools do not teach this wisdom. We can spend years learning how to create wealth but rarely consider how to enjoy it. We can pour enormous resources into a wedding yet never investigate how to give and receive love. Every year we spend millions on looking good but little on learning how to be good. After a lifetime of "productive" labor we often leave the world worse than we found it.

In short, we find ourselves living in a world where materialism and ego dominate rather than spiritualism and altruism. This dominant cultural trait runs counter to the Jewish ideal of pleasure.

But if Judaism advocates pleasure, what is wrong with materialism? Isn't materialism a legitimate form of pleasure?

We answer these questions by differentiating between material and physical. *Physical* refers to aesthetics: the pleasures of the senses. Aesthetic pleasure is an important part of life, along with *emotional, moral,* and *creative* pleasures. Judaism not only advocates the pursuit of these three areas of pleasure, but also considers it an error to deny one or more of them, as they are part of our life's purpose.

We experience each of these four areas either as a material pleasure or a spiritual one. A material pleasure is the enjoyment experienced by the body. A spiritual pleasure is the enjoyment experienced by the soul.

BODY, SOUL, AND AMAZEMENT

This confusion between physical and material results from different theories of the nature of self. Modern culture defines the self in material terms. If my being is essentially material, then my values will be materialistic.

Conversely, if my being is essentially spiritual, then my values will be spiritual ones.

Judaism claims that a person is essentially a soul temporarily fused to a body. The soul is a "spark" of the Infinite Source. Just as the Infinite Source is the quintessence of reality, the human soul is permanent and real. In contrast, the body, a product of the finite material world, is ultimately unreal.

Therefore, the extent to which an experience gives pleasure to the soul is the extent to which it is a "real" pleasure;

the extent to which it gives pleasure to the body is the extent to which it is unreal.

Every type of real pleasure has an unreal, counter-pleasure. For instance, one of the most basic pleasures we know is the enjoyment of good food. A gourmet is a person who has cultivated the aesthetic appreciation for food. This is a spiritual pleasure, for although the body is involved, the actual location of enjoyment is not identifiable within the body. Who knows why many people prefer a fine wine with their meal to a glass of water? We might be able to reduce the wine to its elements, see how the molecules affect the palate, yet we would be no closer to understanding why we enjoy drinking it—a sure sign of a spiritual pleasure. Even one day when phrenologists can identify the exact electrical-chemical activity in the brain that occurs when a person enjoys good food, we still will not understand *why* we enjoy the food.

The antithesis to a gourmet is the person the French call a *gourmand*—one who eats gluttonously, for bodily satisfaction.

There is a constant, unrelenting tension between the two. At any moment, one could choose to unleash the body and devour a chocolate cake. We have all been there so many times we have an expression that "the cookies were calling me." There was a voice calling you to eat the cookies—the voice of your body.

The secret to gourmet eating is to use the body's appetite to energize the eating experience, under the control of a disciplined mind. Like a horse and rider, the ideal relationship is that in which the rider is in control. The horse (the body) provides all the power (in this case, appetite) and the rider (soul) all the direction. The mind makes choices at nearly every waking moment of every day to fulfill the desires of either the body or the soul. Ideally, one would strive to discipline the mind to make soul choices rather than body choices, to be a gourmet rather than a gourmand.

A useful litmus test to know whether a particular choice is being guided by the soul or by the body is to ask: "Is this pleasure that I'm seeking short-term gratification (e.g., I'm hungry, I want food now) or longer-term (I'm going to take an hour to prepare a gourmet meal in order to savor complex aromas and flavors)?" In fact, it is possible to satisfy both body and soul at the same time. But to do so requires that the brain mediate between the two to prevent the body from running out of control.

Unfortunately, exercising the brain comes second only to physical exercise on the list of most detested things to do. This is why true creativity is so rarely found.

> *People will go to any amount of effort to*
> *avoid the labor of thinking.*
> THOMAS JEFFERSON

> *Most people would rather die than think—and most do.*
> BERTRAND RUSSELL

Food and physical consumption is not the only stage of the soul-body dichotomy. It applies to all kinds of pleasure:

- aesthetics v. gluttony
- love and caring v. lust and infatuation
- ethics v. public image
- creativity v. power

The words on the left are the spiritual soul pleasures and the right-hand words are the material body pleasures. Every human experience falls into one of these categories. We must constantly negotiate between the material (body) and the spiritual (soul) impulses:

CONFLICTING MESSAGES FROM BODY AND SOUL

Drive	Material/body message	Spiritual/soul message
Aesthetic	"Let's eat!"	"Make a gourmet meal!"
Love (relationship)	"Procreate!"	"Cultivate the relationship!"
Ethical	"Save face/look good!"	"Do the right thing!"
Creative	"Be successful!"	"Change the world!"

The most important thing to remember is that these messages are constant, like a flowing stream. The body always wants material gratification and the soul always wants spiritual gratification. Just to be mindful of the dichotomy can have lasting spiritual benefits.

Now, as good as it sounds, spiritual gratification is not necessarily transcendent. One may experience the most sublime aesthetic, loving, ethical, and creative pleasures and never transcend the finite realm. Although they are "soul" pleasures, the soul itself remains, after all, attached to the body in this world.

But because of the soul's infinite root, it has the potential to transcend the boundaries set by the finite world. It can do so within the scope of any of the various pleasures. One can, in other words, infuse one's life with transcendental awareness. Such awareness is a unique pleasure in that it by definition transcends all else. This experience is the experience of amazement. Striving toward it is the art of amazement.[2]

Four pleasure areas:	Three pleasure dimensions:
Aesthetics (A)	Material (M)
Love (L)	Spiritual (S)
Ethics (E)	Transcendental (T)
Creativity (C)	

Each item in the left-hand box is a realm of pleasure. Amazement is the vehicle for transforming any and every pleasure from a spiritual one into a transcendental one.

Notice how the contents of the material world (including the body) are necessary agents of spiritual and transcendental experiences. Without the material, we would be unable to experience transcending it.

For example, consider the enjoyment of a sunset. The aesthetic pleasure experienced by my soul cannot happen without eyes to see and a sun to be seen. Because my soul is fused to such a body in such a material world, it is able to experience the aesthetic and transcendental pleasures.

This transcendental access is available via all four areas of pleasure. Any of these areas affords the possibility of all three dimensions of pleasure.

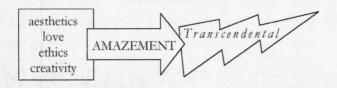

Subsequent chapters will cover each of the four pleasure areas to show how this process works. The reading should be accompanied by doing the practical exercises. Reading this book without doing the exercises would be akin to reading about Beethoven's Ninth Symphony without ever hearing the music—fascinating but not transforming.

THE PLEASURE WAVE

The wave model illustrates the above principles with the added element of hierarchy. For, even in the realm of true, spiritual pleasure, some pleasures are greater than others.

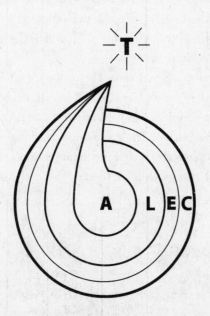

First, consider aesthetic (sensory) pleasure (A): the diagram represents the fact that one can experience a real (meaning spiritual) aesthetic pleasure in itself, but can also use that experience to achieve transcendental pleasure. So, too, for the pleasures of love (L), ethics (E), and creativity (C).

The diagram further represents the fact that the soul's experiences of emotional, ethical, and creative pleasure are increasingly more expansive: they are increasingly higher, or greater, levels of pleasure.

I would like to preempt one point of doubt that often arises. A person who has been raised in modern Western Culture may object to the relatively low status of love on this chart. "But I thought love was the ultimate!" you may object. Sit tight: This challenging point will be demonstrated in subsequent chapters.

This chart does not show the process, that of the metaphorical rider taming the horse. Without a rider, the horse (body) runs rampant. Under control, it can take the soul on an awesome journey. The mind must continually choose between following the body's inclinations to wander into the pastures of materialism or to stay the path that the soul illuminates.

MIND CONTROL AND MEDITATION

Based on this framework, the pursuit of pleasure depends on the simple mental process of distinguishing between material and spiritual impulses (M and S) and on the conscious choice as to which impulse to heed.

The remaining chapters will each focus on one pleasure area (A, L, E, and C): how to distinguish between the M and S of that area and the tools that Judaism gives us to stay the spiritual path by consistently choosing S over M—the art of amazement. For, as we will see, it is this very tension between spiritual and material impulses that makes the deepest amazement possible.

In order to navigate among the competing material (M) and spiritual (S) messages of body and soul, we make conscious mental choices. Therefore, the foundation of pleasure and the basis of Jewish spirituality is the discipline of mental control, of focusing the mind at will. To develop such a discipline requires a systematic development of mental focus, also known as meditation.

> *When a person meditates on these things and recognizes all the creations—from forces, to constellations, to people like oneself— he will be in awe of the wisdom of the Hidden Source in all of its handiworks and all its creations. Pleasurable identification with the Infinite will increase, and one's soul will expand and body will strive to love the Infinite, the Source.*
> RABBI MOSES MAIMONIDES (RAMBAM)[3] (1135–1204)

Ancient Jews understood this role of meditation in spiritual growth with such clarity that meditation became as integral to ancient Israelite culture as television has become to ours.

Jews learned meditation in schools all over ancient Israel.[4] As meditation practices developed over the millennia, the ultimate goal has remained the same—to transcend one's consciousness beyond the mundane, finite here-and-now toward the infinite source of the mundane.

The ancient meditation schools used a curriculum that was specifically tailored toward the achievement of a clear and direct line of communication with the Infinite. Such a level of communication is the ultimate state of transcendental awareness and is called *nevius,* or "prophecy."

PROPHECY: ULTIMATE AMAZEMENT

Prophecy is generally misunderstood. It does not mean simply telling the future. A person who tells the future via naturalistic forces is called a fortune-teller or a soothsayer, an extremely un-Jewish practice, according to the Torah.[5] Since the greatest Jews of history were prophets, they must have been doing something other than (or in addition to) predicting the future.

Part of the misunderstanding of prophecy comes from the fact that the Bible records the prophecies of only forty-eight post-Mosaic prophets, many of whom bring tidings of doom and destruction. No wonder the word *prophet* has become associated with prescience.

In fact, prophecy is defined by an experience rather than by a specific type of pronouncement.[6] We actually know very little about the prophetic experience because true prophecy has been absent from the world since the fourth century B.C.E. Yet the scattered evidence, including descriptive sources, indicates an experience of channeling energy. Please see the Appendix for some of these sources.

The average (nonprophetic) person receives indirect but potentially clear communications from the Infinite in the form of the events that occur to us every day. There are some, particularly certain insane people, who can apparently receive direct but unclear communications.[7] In contrast, the prophetic experience is described as a communication that is both clear and direct.

To reach the prophetic state of consciousness required a long period of study, meditation, and inner purification. To succeed required both tremendous self-discipline and professional guidance. Modern authorities such as Rabbi Joseph Soloveitchik affirm that prophecy is the "ultimate peak" of human creative achievement.[8]

The nationwide system of meditation schools produced, over a period of 500–800 years, more than one million prophets—1,200 or more "graduating" every year. This continual influx created a prophet cadre who acquired an important social role. Imagine, for example, that you had lost your keys. You would have been able to go to the neighborhood prophet for help. He or she might tell you, "Your keys are in your coat pocket. By the way, you've been careless lately—perhaps you should think about why you lost them in the first place?"[9]

In other words, a person who reached the meditative state called prophecy took on a special responsibility to help others grow, too.

Each of us has the potential to achieve prophecy.[10] This handbook alone will not get you there, but the basic skills taught in these lessons are the prerequisite for the journey. The first step is to develop the meditative powers of the mind.

NOTES

1. French, A. P., *Einstein: A Centenary Volume*, p. 53.
2. Philosopher Pierre Hadot has detected a similar spiritual ideal in Greco-Roman philosophy, an ideal he labels "philosophy as a way of life" (see Hadot, *Philosophy as a Way of Life*, Ch. 11). Indeed, spiritual awareness is the ideal of every religion and for some is the definition of religion. The Jewish path is distinguished, aside from its ritual particularities, in its specific philosophic framework, outlined in the previous chapter.
3. *MT Hilchos Yesodei HaTorah* 84:12.
4. See Chapter 1, footnotes 10 and 14.
5. *Leviticus* 19:26, 31; Deuteronomy 18:10–11.
6. Cf Rashbam on Genesis 20:7. The root of the Hebrew *navi* (prophet) is *nun-bet,* which denotes hollowness or openness; to receive transcendental wisdom, one must make oneself "open." See also Luzatto, *Daas Tvunos,* p. 331.
7. *Talmud Baba Basra* 12b.
8. Soloveitchik, Rabbi Joseph B., *Halachic Man.* Trans. Lawrence Kaplan. Philadelphia: Jewish Publication Society, 1991, p. 130.
9. Thanks to Rabbi Shmuel Silinsky for this analogy.
10. *Talmud Avodah Zara* 20b. Cf Luzatto, *Path of the Just,* p. 13.

FOUR

•

MINDFULNESS

The Art of Awareness

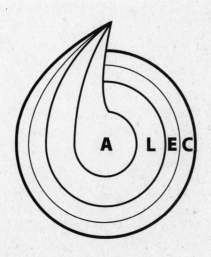

Prepare the Body to Prepare the Mind

Focus the Mind/Contemplation

Developing Constant Focus—
Kavana
Deveikus

❧

The tree that moves some to tears of joy
is in the Eyes of the others only a Green thing
that stands in the way.
WILLIAM BLAKE[1]

PREPARE THE BODY
TO PREPARE THE MIND

The first practice of meditative discipline is surprisingly physical: washing the hands. The idea is to clean the hands both physically and ritually. Physical cleanliness requires, of course, soap and water. Ritual washing comes after physical cleaning. The hands should be free of dirt and other things that inhibit the water from contact with the skin.

What is the meaning of this ritual?

The hands are the main link between our bodies and the

world around us.[2] They are, according to anthropologists, one of the primary physical characteristics that distinguish us as humans. We use our hands for most physical activities.

As our primary physical tool, we relate to our hands in a very physical way. In this context they represent the opposite of spiritual growth. Moreover, because of their constant use, they frequently become soiled.

Therefore, ritual hand washing is an act that declares, "I'm stepping into a spiritual realm now; I'm going to elevate my physical body and actions to a higher plane of consciousness." The custom is to wash at key moments of transition between physical and transcendental, such as upon waking, before eating a meal, and before certain kinds of meditation.[3]

The function of ritual is widely misunderstood.

Ritual is not magic and is not merely a psychological tool. Psychologically, when we perform a ritual act, we are indeed adding meaning to an otherwise ordinary motion. But we are doing much more.

Recall the theme of Chapter 2: the Infinite is by definition absolute reality and this world is somewhat illusory. The simplest metaphor to illustrate this theme is the difference between the light of a movie projector and the image on the screen.

When we watch a movie, what are we actually seeing? There is a bulb, which emits a light, which passes through a film, reflects off a screen, and reaches our eyes. The film produces dark patches that trick our eyes into thinking that we are viewing real images; in fact, we see only one light.

In this analogy, the light is the Infinite—an infinite light. The images we "see" are the material world around us. We become engrossed in the movie and believe it is quite real—which it is, but not in the way it seems. These multiple things (images) do not really exist—they are illusions produced by the selective filtering of the single light.

If the Infinite Light is the ultimate reality, then actions that are confined to the finite world are ultimately unreal. The only events in this world that are real are those that somehow transcend the finite world and connect to or reveal the Infinite reality. Therefore, when one properly performs a spiritual action, the person, action, and object are all literally transformed from unreal to real—assuming one has the right mental focus.[4]

Therefore, a transcendental ritual such as washing the hands has the potential to be an action of utmost creativity, transforming the illusory to the real.

The details of this ritual, like much of our meditative tradition, are based on practices in King Solomon's Temple. Hand washing recalls the priests preparing for their service. But washing the hands is not simply a commemoration. Even while the Temple stood, Jews washed their hands upon rising, before a meal, when leaving a cemetery, among other things. The public Temple and its service have always served as a model for the individual path.

EXERCISE

Try the hand-washing ritual upon rising for one week.

Directions:

1. Fill a large glass (or any smooth-rimmed container) with water.
2. Make sure that the hands are visibly clean.
3. Consider the fact that you are in transition from material to spiritual awareness.
4. Pour water alternately over right and left hands, three times each. Each pouring should cover the fingers completely and most of the hand (ideally to the wrist).
5. Dry hands well.

After one week, try the hand washing at other times of the day, such as before meditation.

•

FOCUS THE MIND/CONTEMPLATION

Each category of pleasure requires a specific type of mental effort borne out of the pleasure itself. For instance, aesthetic pleasure requires that one pay attention to the desired sensory experience. When the mind wanders, it experiences no pleasure from the immediate experience. Consider the game of basketball: the physical and mental exertion can be a great pleasure; yet, when a player becomes distracted by pain, worries, thoughts of a loved one, or any other thoughts, the enjoyment of the game itself decreases. Moreover, the level of play will be diminished, further lowering the pleasure.

Pleasure depends, therefore, on focus. This observation reveals why people seek new and exhilarating experiences. Our minds have become so dulled that we need situations of novelty, danger, and excitement to derive the same attentive pleasure that a child finds in a leaf or an ant.

Alternatively, we can develop the mind's ability to focus. The simplest method is to practice focusing on an external object.

EXERCISE — PRACTICE
CONTEMPLATION

Choose a natural object such as a flower or a leaf (an artifact like a pen or a cup will work, if necessary). Choose a time and place where you can sit without interruption. For five minutes, intently examine the object. Study it: notice its colors, shape, texture, smell, and taste. Consider its form and function—how do they correspond? How do they correlate?

Finally, behold the object at arm's length and contemplate it as a whole. Where did it come from? How did it get from there to your hand?

•

Proper contemplation leads to a deeper appreciation of the object. Over time, the practice leads the mind to seek the source of the object—first physical and then metaphysical sources. Eventually, the five-minute meditation should result in the mind in active pursuit of the Infinite.

The practice of contemplation resembles learning to play a musical instrument. Imagine a novice who wants to play the piano. She never before touched a piano, but she heard a piece by Chopin and wants to play it, so she sits down at the piano. What will happen? Well, unless she is a prodigy not much is going to happen. She must start with one note at a time and practice consistently to develop the skill. Eventually, with discipline and perseverance, most people could probably play Chopin—*if they put their mind to it.*

> *A fool sees not the same tree that a wise man sees.*
> WILLIAM BLAKE

Contemplation is an exercise to help you develop the mind's ability to focus on something. Most people find that it is not easy to focus on one thing exclusively even for five minutes.

EXERCISE

1. Choose a time and place to practice a daily contemplation-meditation. Do it for a week. After the first week, do exercise #2.

2. Contemplation-meditation is called *hisbonenus* (*hitbonenut*), which literally means "building oneself." Based on your experience doing *hisbonenus*, explain the relationship between contemplating external objects and self-development.

•

DEVELOPING CONSTANT FOCUS—*KAVANA*

In the long term, *hisbonenus* develops a mind that can focus at will in various settings. This is the most basic mental skill and the secret to success in many human endeavors, such as:

- speed reading
- musical proficiency
- an athlete's "mental game"
- play (recreation)
- sleep

In Hebrew, focused attention is called *kavana*. It comes from the root *koon*, which means "directness" or "correctness," and the same root is found in the Hebrew words for "to intend," "to prepare," "ready," and "correct." Rabbi Samson Raphael Hirsch links these words to the two-letter root *kayn*—"yes," suggesting that *kavana* has something to do with affirmation.[5] Abraham and Rachel Witty translate *kavana* elegantly as a "spirit of sincere devotion."[6]

The following exercises will enhance your skill of *kavana*. Enhanced general *kavana* naturally leads to greater *kavana* in life situations such as those above. It will also greatly assist you in later lessons of this book.

The development of *kavana* clearly involves a tremendous shift of perspective as one moves from automatic pilot toward greater awareness and active control. Taking steps to cause such a shift is what is known as becoming a spiritual person.

EXERCISES TO ENHANCE AWARENESS

1. *Develop self-awareness*: Make a list of five actions that you do every day and start a daily record of your level of *kavana* in each action, on a scale of 1 to 10. Keep this record for one week.

2. *Sense-awareness*: Make five columns or lists, one for each of the five senses, and notice one new thing per day for each sense. Pay attention to colors, smells, and shapes. Appreciate the details of the world around you. Keep this record for one week.

3. *Habits*: become aware of a routine by *doing an action by routine,* such as placing money into your pocket. Why this pocket and not the other one? Why take this route and not another? Take notice of a routine action you perform and bring awareness to it. For example, while brushing your teeth, notice each action and sensation—the weight of the toothbrush, the texture of the bristles, squeezing

the paste, the sound of the water, the taste
and smell. . . .

4. *Catch yourself switching to automatic pilot,* unaware, day-
   dreaming, and fidgeting. If you want to daydream,
   then make a decision to do so. But don't let yourself slip into a dream automatically, as soon as you
   sit down in the metro, set off on a walk, etc. (This
   category includes all forms of laziness—lying in
   bed longer than you need to, watching too much
   TV, and so on.) Bring awareness to the action and
   notice the results.

•

The goal of Chapter 2 was to grasp and internalize the
philosophy that the Infinite is the source of everything and
in fact is all that really exists, despite our sensory perceptions.

In Chapter 3, we defined the dual nature of the human
being. The tension between the two natures can generate
tremendous energy. The key to pleasure in life is to harness
that energy.

In the present chapter we have developed the founda-
tions of *kavana.* When we experience the physical world at even
the most basic levels of *kavana,* such as contemplating a leaf,
we are transcending our ordinary perception of the world.
Transcendence is not some place in the mind that takes years
to discover. It is available immediately with a little effort.

Every beginner to contemplative exercises knows that even the initial, unpracticed transcendental experience is vastly richer than that of one who makes no effort. And the transcendental experience grows: week by week of daily practice, one's awareness should become sharper.

The natural result of progress in this area is a mind that is more "present"—i.e., aware of the present moment and the world around me right now.

DEVEIKUS

After beginning to develop the basic mental power of *kavana*, the next step is to apply this mental skill to the philosophy of Chapter 2, namely, to pursue the constant awareness of the Infinite's presence in every place and at every moment.

Such awareness, even when temporary, is called *deveikus (deveikut)*, which means "connecting" or "attachment" (in modern Hebrew, *devek* means "glue"). To have a constant awareness of the Infinite is what it means "to connect" or to attach oneself to the Infinite.[7] Hence, the psalmist writes,

I have set the Infinite before me always . . . (Psalms 16:8)

This verse has long been understood as a reference to constant awareness.[8]

EXERCISE

In ancient times, the psalms were used for meditation. Some of these meditations concern the act of meditation itself. Consider verses 12–13 from Psalm 51:

A pure heart create for me, Infinite Manifestation in Nature,
*   and a spirit of kavana renew within me;*
Don't cast me away from before you and the spirit of your
*   Transcendence don't take from me.*

What is the Psalmist saying about *kavana* and *deveikus*?

•

NOTES

1. Blake, William, "From Letter to Revd. Dr. Trusler (23 August 1799) in Duncan Wu (ed.), *Anthology of Romanticism* (2nd Ed.), Oxford: Blackwell, 1998, p. 114.
2. *Talmud Brachos 15a; Talmud Sukka 26b;* cf Commentaries of Rashba and Rosh there.
3. *Shulchan Aruch Orach Chaim* 92:4,5 and *Mishna Berura* 13. Also before and after marital relations; some also wash ritually after relieving themselves. See also *Mishna Berura* 92:25; *Pri Magaden* 92:4; *Shulchan Aruch Orach Chaim* 233:2; *Tor* 92.
4. In Deuteronomy 4:29 the verb changes from plural (*bikashtem/you*

sought) to singular (*matsasa/you found* and *sidr'shenu/you will search*), which the Vilna Gaon interprets thus: only those individuals who "will search" will find; i.e., not all spiritual seekers succeed, only those with the appropriate mental focus. Cf *Talmud Rosh Hashana* 18a.

5. Hirsch wrote a Biblical commentary that is available in several editions (see Bibliography); see Hirsch's comment to Exodus 2:14.

6. Witty, *Exploring Jewish Tradition,* p. 60.

7. Cf Ibn Ezra on Deuteronomy 10:20 and 11:22, and Ramban there. Alternatively, Rashi there opines that the way to *deveikus* is to spend time with Torah scholars.

8. See Rashi, Ibn Ezra, and Meztuda on Psalms 16:8.

FIVE

•

HEAVEN IN
A WILDFLOWER

The Art of Appreciation

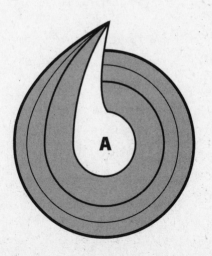

To see the world in a grain of sand
and a heaven in a wild flower,
Hold infinity in the palm of your hand
and eternity in an hour.

WILLIAM BLAKE

True *deveikus,* or mental and emotional attachment, to the Infinite does not merely feel right and complete. It is by definition the most real experience one can have in this world. Because *deveikus* is so wonderful, beautiful, and real, it should be a daily goal—not a disconnected, specialized experience, but an awareness of life in all of its details.

This *deveikus* is a specific transcendental level. Ultimately, recalling Chapter 2, the Infinite's essence is unknowable by a finite mind with finite senses. Nonetheless, the Infinite created this universe for the purpose of giving to another; we are that other and the greatest gift to us is the ability to have a relationship with the Infinite itself. This is a paradox—how can we have a relationship to something that we cannot sense or imagine?

The answer brings us back to the paradox of Chapter 2: at the moment of the big bang, when the finite world came into being, did the Infinite thereby cease to be infinite? After all, now we have an Infinite and a finite which are somehow separate. If so, then how can we still call it "infinite"? If not, if it remains totally infinite and not separate from the finite, how come we only perceive "finite-ness" around us?

In other words, where is the Infinite in relation to the finite?

Another way of asking the question is: From our point of view, we understand that the universe was created about thirteen billion years ago. But when was it created from the Infinite's "perspective," as it were—given that we define the Infinite as existing before the big bang, therefore beyond time? What are the ontological implications of "beginning of time"?

HOW INFINITE AND FINITE COEXIST

Since by definition the Infinite cannot cease to be infinite, from its perspective the universe was created . . . just now. And now. And now. . . . At every moment (as we perceive time) the Infinite continues to create or cause finite existence.

This resolution of the paradox should clarify the meaning of omnipresence—it is inaccurate to describe the Infinite as "in everything" (as people often say that "God is in me and you"). The diametric opposite is true: Everything is in the Infinite. The Infinite is the "location" of the universe. Indeed, one of the Hebrew terms for the Infinite is *ha-Makom*—"the Place."

On human terms, however, it suffices to understand that the Infinite by definition is always very near to us.[1] This understanding is not intellectually difficult but does require practice to develop into a constant awareness.

In the East, the practice of constant focus and awareness is the central practice of Zen Buddhism.[2] Westerners developed a limited version of this awareness called epiphany: the momentary experience of an object's infinite source.

Judaism combines the two: to cultivate both an expanded mind and a constant awareness. The practitioner of Jewish "transcendental" meditation seeks to perceive the Infinite's manifestation in everything finite and through all of life's experiences.[3]

It is easiest to realize transcendental *deveikus* when experiencing natural phenomena or great physical exertion. But we cannot see sunsets every minute of the day, not even every day. (If we could, we might not need meditation; we could just sit back and . . . transcend.) Life is mundane on the surface and in order to make that connection and to have that experience of *wow!* as often as possible we need a meditative discipline.

It is in search of this *wow!* experience that many people have resorted to ingesting chemicals. Mind-altering drugs sharpen the senses and enhance the details of life. Aside from unpleasant side effects, including addiction, these artificial methods are ultimately self-defeating because they weaken the mind rather than strengthen it. With long-term use, the drugs destroy the very senses that they were supposed to enhance. This painful result has been given the apt name of burnout.

Jewish spirituality works very much in the opposite direction. It is based entirely on the use and development of the mind and the senses. Thus, with long-term practice it strengthens the mind significantly. Long-term practitioners report an enviable level of enjoyment of life.

Another benefit of meditation over artificial mind-expanders is that meditation is significantly cheaper! It requires neither artificial chemicals nor a radical change in lifestyle. It does not require any particular personality type.

EXERCISE

If you ever had an experience where your senses were altered by an artificial substance, write a comparison of that experience to the previous lesson's exercises in sharpening your natural perception.

•

Transcendental amazement meditation does require a desire to transcend the mundane. It requires mental and emotional effort. For long-term success, it requires self-discipline. For the beginner, above all, it requires an adventurous spirit.

The following exercise builds on the introductory *kavana* practice in the previous chapter.

HOW TO EAT A PIECE OF FRUIT

Find two pieces of the same kind of fruit. Try to choose something fragrant, such as ripe oranges. If it is not orange season, take any fresh, juicy fruit—grapes, pears, watermelon, etc. Before continuing, eat one of the pieces of fruit. It is important not to read ahead until you do this exercise.

Take the second piece of fruit. Hold it in your hand and notice as many of its features as you can: shapes, textures, colors, smells, tastes, sounds (as you manipulate it). It is not necessary to describe it out loud or to enumerate its features. Just notice them. If you run out of features to notice, go back over those that you already noticed. Go over the fruit like a detective. Also, in addition to its fine details, notice the larger features. Notice the fact that it has a protective skin. Notice that its attractive color and smell produce an emotional or even physiological reaction in you.

Now, contemplate all that happened in order for this piece of fruit to come into your hand. Many crucial agents were essential for the delivery of this fruit:

> money bought it . . .
> a grocer supplied it . . .
> a delivery system got it to the grocer . . .
> a farmer harvested it . . .
> a tree produced it . . .
> the rain helped the tree . . .
> solar energy brought the rain and fueled the tree . . .

But where did the sun get its energy? While the sun has been shining for a very long time, astronomers believe that it did have an origin. Ultimately, the sun's nuclear fusion—and all energy in the universe—came from the big bang. And the big bang came from the Infinite.

So now we see a direct chain, from the Infinite to this fruit in your hand.

Imagine you were sitting on the board of the Ford Foundation, one of the greatest sponsors of scientific research. One day, another board member holds up a piece of fruit and declares, "Ladies and gentlemen, this year I want to fund the production of these in a test tube, from scratch." How much are you going to invest? How much would it cost in research dollars to produce such a fruit from scratch in the laboratory? Millions?

The answer is that it cannot currently be done. No amount of money could create such a technology in the foreseeable future. If it could, the price would be in the billions. From this perspective, the orange is essentially priceless. Even one hypothetical day when we will be able to create fruit without seeds and soil, it will be after astronomical developmental costs. Yet today, with little cost or effort, you are holding one in your hand.

And furthermore, if you pause to think for even a minute, you may realize how strange it is that you are even able to hold such a piece of fruit, that your hand does what you want it to do, and that you desire such a piece of fruit, that you have these olfactory glands and taste buds that somehow communicate information to your brain that translates into pleasure. . . .

How did you create the karma[4] to deserve such a precious gift?

As you contemplate the fruit and its history, you should begin to develop a greater appreciation for it. If you contemplate it long enough, your appreciation should develop into joy—joy from the existence of such beauty, joy from thankfulness that you are able to experience such beauty. What an incredible gift.

When you begin to feel joy, eat the fruit. Take your time. Close your eyes.

As you chew, concentrate on the taste and texture. Chew slowly. Swallow deliberately.

EXERCISE

Describe the difference between eating the first and second pieces of fruit.

•

If you did this exercise carefully, including the specific details, you should have gained a deep understanding of the spiritual potential of any aesthetic experience.

According to Judaism, since the Infinite is the source of this universe it is necessarily the source of every detail of the fruit and of every step of the fruit's production and delivery. Therefore, the ultimate step in basic amazement meditation is to experience the fruit (and all other sensory experiences) with the awareness that the experience is an intimate encounter with the Infinite. Recall the principle of the universe as a wavelength of the Infinite. When you eat an orange with both appreciation of its details and awareness of its source, you have reached a significant level of transcendence.

To solidify and deepen the connection requires remembering, while contemplating and eating the fruit, that it is a gift. Imagine how you might feel if a dear friend arrived with a personalized gift. Moreover, this particular gift saves your life! For without food, one would literally die: the soul would separate from the body. Food, then, is the primary "glue" that keeps the soul in the body. How can one not think: *What did I do to deserve such beauty?*

By now, many people's appreciation for the fruit becomes so deep that it brings tears to the eyes. If you are such a person, do not fight the tears—let them flow. If you are not so emotional, you are not necessarily lacking. You may be a person who expresses emotions differently. The important thing is practice focusing on the qualities of your food until the eating experience becomes an emotional experience as well.

CONSTANT APPRECIATION

Judaism teaches us to take every bite of food with such intense awareness and appreciation.[5] Moreover, we should consume all of our sensory experiences with such awareness and appreciation: everything we hear, see, smell, taste, and touch.

The problem is, for most people it is exceedingly hard to maintain this degree of awareness and appreciation every time one eats.

Similarly, advanced students sometimes ask, "I've succeeded to enhance the experience of eating good food, even to the point where the appreciation of the beauty of the gift makes me smile uncontrollably. But how can I have a transcendental experience when I'm eating food that is not so sweet?"

First of all, eat foods that taste good. Avoid bland or bitter foods whenever possible. Second, most of the food we eat has something pleasant about it. It may have a pleasant texture. Or it may be pleasant simply in the fact that it satisfies hunger. So in most cases, we should be able to appreciate something about the food.

But what about bitter pills and medicines? For that matter, what about any painful experience? Is pain an exception to the rule of constant amazement?

Rather than being an exception, pain is also a gift. It can take months or years of contemplation and growth to appreciate pain. For example, I know a man who developed multiple sclerosis at the young age of forty-five. He was a professional musician and music was central to his life, yet the disease made it extremely painful for him to walk, let alone play his instrument. He went into early retirement from his career as a music teacher. At first he was dismayed—how would life be the same again? Over a period of two years, he learned to play his instrument *with* the pain, and, despite it, he told me that the pain taught him to play better! And now that he had retired, he had more time than ever before to play.

This man's struggle was not uncommon; his success was. Seekers of higher awareness actually find that the distinction between pain and pleasure diminishes until the point when there is no difference! It is hard to imagine, but that is the goal.

This is not a condemnation of pain. Pain is a very useful tool of biofeedback. But we can reach a level where we appreciate pain and are thankful for it just as we are for sweet pleasures. It is a gift to help us on our transcendental path.[6]

Moreover, pain becomes a greater gift when one has developed *kavana* as presented in the previous lesson. For pain is usually largely beyond our control. One who has developed *kavana* will be able to experience pain as much a witness as a victim and thereby experience and learn from the pain as a part of a full life.

Transcendental Amazement

The discussion until now has covered the most basic meditative experiences and presented exercises to develop this constant awareness. Hopefully you have been keeping up with these exercises. When one keeps pace, each lesson of this handbook unfolds like a series of doorways down a long corridor.

In trying the exercises, you probably came upon a barrier. Most people find it relatively easy to find that momentary *wow!*—even on a daily basis. However, we all find it more difficult to sustain the experience of constant awareness and appreciation for more than a few moments at a time, let alone hours or days.

To illustrate this point, I often show an audience a striking photograph of a sunset. In the photo, the light appears to fan outward from the sun in the shape of a light bulb. Once everyone has noticed this unusual feature, I explain, "This is a sunset that no one has ever seen. This photo was taken on Mars."

Inevitably the room reverberates with appreciative "ooohs" and "mmmms."

Then I ask (with feigned annoyance), "Why do you say 'oooh' to this but not to the sound of birds chirping? Or children's laughter? Or to a disposable plastic cup? Or to any of the thousands of astonishing things that we experience every day?"

The answer is obvious—because we have become used to such phenomena. A thoughtful person will agree that the world is full of amazing details—too many! So many that not only would it be impossible to pay attention to all of them, but the very attempt to do so may even be hazardous, such as, for instance, when driving a car or preparing food.

Jewish tradition acknowledges the reality that both extremes are unworkable. One the one hand, total absorption in minuscule details is not practical: our sense of a normal life requires tuning out 99 percent of the information that reaches our senses. On the other hand, to be 100 percent on automatic pilot is the antithesis of the spiritual path.

The middle ground of *kavana* is one of total focus and appreciation of the beautiful world *with which we interact* and acknowledgment of its infinite source.[7]

The reason that the transcendental experience is so elusive is because the mundane, material world is so pervasive. We are, after all, creatures of physical habit. We have material needs and desires every day that tend to draw our minds back to the mundane almost as quickly as we try to transcend that mundane.

Fortunately, human beings come equipped with several tools that are firmly rooted in the material but which has a spiritual aspect, thus bridging the gap between mundane and mystical.

One such tool is the mind. The mind's seat in the material brain makes it possible to affect it by material devices such as chemicals. However, the mind is so spiritual that it is exceedingly difficult to control. In order to guide the mind, we use a related mundane-mystical device, the voice.

USING THE VOICE

The voice employs sounds to concretize that which is happening in the mind, whether intellectual or emotional. While the mind has many physical senses to receive information, it expresses its own processes primarily through the voice. The voice turns the mental and mystical into something material.[8]

The Torah frequently refers to the power of words. The process of tuning in to our spiritual selves sensitizes us to this power and we become careful with our speech. In contrast, we have seen the general decline of word sensitivity in modern societies. Speech standards have become more and more informal. This decline is unfortunate because it hinders the creation of an environment conducive to spiritual development.

The power of speech implies that although all words are equal, some are more equal than others. All words are equal in the sense that any words in any language have a latent transcendental potential. Yet some words are more equal in that some languages seem better suited to make the translation between mystical and mundane.[9]

Hebrew is one such language. According to Jewish tradition, classical Hebrew is the ultimate transcendental language.[10] It was the primordial language spoken by the first person to achieve prophecy, whom the Torah calls Adam. Hebrew has a poetic purity in which there are no exact synonyms and every sentence has the potential to convey multiple meanings when constructed properly.

Our problem today—indeed, of the past 2,400 years—is that we have lost the ability to tap the full potential of the language. The ancients could achieve great transcendental access by simply speaking from the heart. That's the power of the Hebrew tongue when used properly. A language is a tool, and Hebrew is like a key to unlock the doors of transcendence—if one knows how to use it.

General knowledge of Hebrew declined in the fifth and

fourth centuries B.C.E. during and after the Babylonian exile.[11] In response, a congress of sages remembered as the
Great Assembly took historic steps to make user-friendly
transcendental paths available to the general populace. They
composed a series of Hebrew word combinations that would
be less personal than a spontaneous meditation, but that
would allow future generations to access the power of Hebrew and to use it for what I have been calling amazement
meditation. These word combinations are called *brachos/bra-
chot* (singular: *bracha*), a word which at its root refers to a
source or a spring.[12]

(Many readers will recognize the word *bracha* and even
the wording of some of the *brachos*. If you are such a reader,
you may find yourself thinking, Aha—now I understand this
book: this is all a sneaky way to get me to say blessings!

I'm not sure what a blessing is, but I am sure that our understanding of *brachos* has become as distorted as our conception of "God." Try to avoid the pitfall of applying your prior
experience with *brachos* to the art of amazement. Can you recall the radical difference between eating the two pieces of
fruit? There should be a similar radical difference between
the way you used to think of a *bracha* and what you are learning now.

The dilution of Judaism over time has left us a warped
understanding of *bracha*. We would best scrap our preconcep-
tions and begin here from scratch. Do so, and you will find a
radically new Judaism and a real gateway to spirituality.)

ANATOMY OF A *BRACHA*

Brachos are tools for transcendence. They are not transcendence itself. Like all meditations, they do not work by magic. A person who utters them casually will gain little.[13] But when said with understanding and *kavana,* they become a daily source of transcendental amazement.[14]

The *bracha* thereby resolves our dilemma of how to sustain the transcendental experience; how to walk through life in total amazement. We may not achieve that level of *kavana* all day long, but we can certainly reach it whenever we eat.

In the parlance of R. Chaim Velozhin (early nineteenth century), just as food helps the soul connect to the body (because without food, eventually the soul will separate from the body), *brachos* connect the soul to the Infinite.[15]

Ideally, we should all compose our own *brachos* as needed, and such was the practice in early Jewish history. However, the social-political decline that led to the Babylonian conquest paralleled a spiritual decline. This spiritual decay was characterized by, among other things, a loss of sensitivity to the language. The Great Assembly therefore codified the *brachos* in order to perpetuate them. Today it is considered improper to compose one's own *bracha* both because of our general insensitivity to the nuances of the Hebrew language and because we still need common texts to help preserve Jewish unity.

Although one might think that a standardized text limits

creativity, in fact it can be a vehicle for greater creativity. Consider each *bracha* like a classical sonata. Each of us is a musician, and the creative possibilities are as numerous as the number of musicians. Like music, *brachos* should be vocalized, not confined to the imagination. Music is the purest expression of emotions and great music can profoundly affect the emotions. Similarly, speech is the concretization of thought; hence one can control thoughts via speech. A *bracha* is a prophetic sound bite that (for most people) must be vocalized to be effective as a meditation.

Most *brachos* follow the same general pattern.

First, they begin with words that convey the idea of opening a transcendental connection: *"Baruch atah . . ."*

"Baruch" is related to the word *bracha,* and it indicates the source of this moment's life experience. *"Atah"* means "you"— a very personal, endearing appellation for the Infinite! So the *brachos* begin, in translation, "You are the Source . . ."

We use the second person because we humans tend to be drawn to those who are familiar to us. Someone to whom I refer as "you" is immediately closer to me than someone to whom I refer as "he." Therefore, although we're talking *about* the Infinite and not having a conversation, the mystics gave us *brachos* in the language that people speak to one another. The meditation is thereby real and personal.

Next, most *brachos* continue with four names, each of which is an attempt to grasp the Infinite within the limits of the human mind. The four words move the speaker from the most obvious to the most sublime:

ADONOY—*that which was, is, and will ever be*
ELOHAYNU—*our power, the underlying force in nature*[16]
MELECH—*director, pulling the metaphorical puppet strings*
HA-OLAM—*the finite world, "concealing" the Infinite*

All together, the typical *bracha* begins:

> *You are the source—that which was, is, and will ever be—our*
> *power, director of the concealment . . .*

The remainder of the *bracha* specifies the experience at hand. If the experience is eating a piece of fruit, then the *bracha* ends with ". . . creating fruit." Indeed, the four appellations listed above describe a force that surely does create fruit and everything else in life.

Altogether, the *bracha* is a meditative phrase that aids us in focusing on that piece of fruit and appreciating every aspect of it, including the fact that it exists at all and that I am able to enjoy it!

It is crucial to avoid the misconception that the fruit is infinite, or worse, that the fruit is *the* Infinite. More accurately—to the extent that our language will allow—the fruit is *of* the Infinite. The Infinite is there, but then again, it's everywhere. We can choose to eat the fruit in a way that will help us expand our awareness of the Infinite's infiniteness. The *bracha* is thereby a very useful tool to steer our normal perception toward a transcendental one.

Since each *bracha* addresses a single, isolated experience, in order to infuse one's entire life with amazement, one should try to use *brachos* in conjunction with the full range of life experiences.

This is in fact exactly what the Great Assembly codified. They wrote *brachos* for many kinds of experiences conducive to capturing a *wow!* in order to use those moments to transcend the finite. Their goal was to give the individual a tool to make daily mundane events into mystical experiences.

The Great Assembly included Israel's wisest sages, among them three Biblical prophets: Haggai, Zechariah, and Malachi.[17] With prophetic insight into both human nature and the Hebrew language, they created *brachas* to be used when awaking and when retiring, when eating and when relieving, when putting on shoes and when greeting a long-lost friend, when witnessing natural phenomena, when giving birth, and when encountering death.[18]

For instance, there are different *brachos* for various food types. There is a special *bracha* for seeing lightning and another for hearing thunder. There is a *bracha* for seeing a rainbow. There is a special *bracha* for a parent holding a newborn baby for the first time. There is a special *bracha* for seeing an unusually beautiful person or animal. There is another *bracha* for seeing an unusually ugly, deformed creature (that comes from the same source, after all).[19] There is a *bracha* for unusually good news, and a different *bracha* for unusually bad news.[20] There is a special *bracha* for seeing a world-class secular scholar (*"Wow—Stephen Hawking!"*). There is even a special *bracha* for going to the bathroom (*"I can hold it in, and I can let it out—amazing!"*).

When the Infinite has given you a large amount of possessions, do not forget to be thankful for even the minor items . . . given you.
RABBI MOSHE FEINSTEIN[21]

Brachos are so beneficial to expanding one's consciousness that the Talmud recommends saying one hundred per day.[22] Divide a typical sixteen-hour day by one hundred and the result is, on average, a *bracha* every ten minutes. Although practically speaking it is easier to cluster them together at certain times throughout the day, the overall effect of striving for one hundred is to pepper the day with the kind of meditative moments of appreciation that *brachos* so successfully create.

The Great Assembly had a secondary goal as well. The Babylonian conquest seventy years earlier had scattered Jews to several parts of the world where they adopted new mother tongues. This demographic dispersion has persisted for 2,400 years. To this day, only a minority of Jews live in Israel and speak Hebrew (which linguistically has evolved from Biblical Hebrew sufficiently to call it a different tongue). As a counterforce, the canonization of a common liturgy had the effect of maintaining Jewish spiritual unity despite the geographic and cultural dispersion.

The primary building block of that common spirituality is the *bracha*, which answers the challenge of materialism. The material world presents us with two choices. First, we must choose every day and every moment whether to enjoy it as a gourmet (spiritually) or as a glutton (materially). Second, we choose whether to enjoy it only in itself, or to use

the aesthetic experience to leap toward transcendental awareness. The *bracha* is a user-friendly method for elevating the
aesthetic experience into the *wow!* that it should be.

EXERCISES

1. Choose one *bracha* from the following list and say it
   with *kavana* once a day for a week.

2. Learn one new *bracha* every week and use it whenever appropriate. Continue to the next lesson after
   you've learned and used at least four *brachos* to your
   satisfaction.

Each *bracha* begins with:

"Baruch atah ADONOY elohaynu melech ha-olam . . ."
You are the source—that which was, is, and will ever be—our
   power, director of the concealment . . .

Event	Bracha
hearing thunder, experiencing an earthquake, tornado, etc.	. . . sheh kocho uge-vuraso malay olam. (. . . whose power and might fill the world.)

seeing lightning, a comet, a snow-capped mountain for the first time after thirty days or more	. . . osay ma'aseh v'rayshees. (. . . continually doing the original action of creation ex nihilo.)
hearing exceptionally good news shared by two or more people	. . . ha tov v'ha mayteev. (. . . the good and the doer of good.)
hearing exceptionally bad news (customarily said only on the death of a parent, God forbid)	. . . dayan ha-emes. (. . . the true judge.)
seeing the ocean after at least thirty days	. . . osay hayam hagadol. (. . . making the great sea.)
eating fruit	. . . boray pree ha-ayts. (. . . creating the fruit of the tree.)

eating vegetables	. . . boray pri ha-adama. (. . . creating the fruit of the ground.)
drinking wine or grape juice	. . . boreh pree ha-gafen. (. . . creating the fruit of the vine.)
drinking most beverages; eating animal products	. . . sheh-hakol ni-he-yeh bidvaroh. (. . . that everything comes from its essence.)
seeing exceptionally beautiful trees or creatures	. . . sheh cha-cha lo b'olamo. (. . . that even *this* is in its world.)
seeing an exception-ally deformed person	. . . m'shaneh ha-brios. (. . . that varies the creatures.)
seeing an excep-tional secular scholar	. . . sheh nasan may-chochma-so l'basar v'dam. (. . . that gave of its wisdom to flesh and blood.)

purchasing a new	. . . sheh-hekianu,
house, furniture,	v'keey'manu,
clothes, etc.; eating	v'higianu lahz-mahn
a fruit for the first	hah-zeh. (. . . that
time this season;	kept us alive, and sus-
seeing a loved one	tained us, and brought
after thirty days or	us to this season.)
more of no communi-	
cation	•

Notice that the tagline of every *bracha* is expressed in the present tense. This detail helps us be mindful of the concept that for a finite world to exist it must be continually "made" or sustained by its Infinite source. From our perspective, the universe may be billions of years old, but from an Infinite "perspective" (whatever that may mean, exactly), the universe was created right now. And now! And now. . . .[23]

NOTES

1. Awareness of this concept is the essence of the verse in the Torah that is known in English as the first of the "10 Command-ments"—traditionally called the "10 Statements"; cf Exodus 20:2.
2. Compare the Zen Buddhist tenet of "big mind."
3. Mahayana Buddhism has a similar concept, Bodhidharma, or "Buddhist nature." There are several significant differences, how-ever, between the Buddhist and Jewish ideals. First, as discussed in Chapter 2, whereas Jewish Meditation is totally focused on stretching to infinity, to elevating the material world, including

its pains, Buddhism's goal is the escape from the suffering of the material world.

Second, for a Buddhist to develop Bodhidharma can take many years, but for a serious student of Jewish Meditation, the meditative state described in this chapter will come in a matter of weeks.

4. "Karma," an English word borrowed from Sanskrit, refers to the principle of cause and effect in both the physical and metaphysical planes of existence. The Jewish concept is called *mida kneged mida*, literally, "measure for measure." The concept will be developed in Chapters 5 and 6.

5. For an idea of the importance of eating in Judaism, consider that the very first commandment in the Torah regards eating (Genesis 2:16), and improper eating is linked to death (Genesis 2:17). For the antidote, see Isaiah 25:26.

6. Velozhin, R. Chaim, *Nefesh HaChaim*, Ch. 1.

7. Rambam (Rabbi Moses Maimonides), *Mishna Torah, Sefer HaMitzvos*, Mitzva 3; *Sefer Mada* 2:1–2.

8. Velozhin, R. Chaim, *Nefesh HaChaim*, 1:13. Technological developments have enabled us to express our thoughts with other media, such as writing, art, music, etc. However, the voice remains the primary, meaning primal, mode of human expression.

9. See *MB* 62:3. See also *Mishna Sotah* 7:1 (*Talmud Sotah* 32a).

10. See Munk, *The Wisdom in the Hebrew Alphabet* (Mesorah, 1993).

11. These traditional Jewish dates do not jibe with traditional archaeological dating. However, the "New Archaeology" has added approximately 150 years to the timeline, bringing it in sync with the traditional Jewish dates. See David Rohl, *Pharaohs and Kings* (Three Rivers Press, 1997).

12. Rashi on *Talmud Sotah* 10a ("B'meh birchu") states: "Every 'bracha' in the Torah denotes increase, something that causes increase and by which fulfillment is found"; Avudraham, p. 33. Cf Ecclesiastes 2:6. Hirsch understood the essence of *bracha* to be the concept of spurring new growth, which is exactly the function of a source.

13. Lunzano, pp. 96–100. Cf R' Yosef Yuzpa Kashman, *Noheg Katzone Yosef,* p. 40.

14. One of the most famous Jewish Hindus, Richard Alpert (aka Ram Dass) described a similar process; yet notice his different goal: "What I mean by the word consecration is bringing into consciousness the nature of the act in a cosmic plan. For example, in the old days people would say grace. Grace was a thing you waited for before you ate the turkey. Norman Rockwell characterizes the kid reaching while everybody's head's bowed. It's that time, 'Let's say grace.' 'Grace.' Now, when I bless food, the statement I say, when I say grace, is an old Sanskrit one. It means 'This offering of this little ritual I'm performing, this is part of it all, part of Brahma, part of that which is eternally all. He who is making the offering means, that which is being offered is part of it all. The hunger to which you are feeding . . . the fare which you are feeding, that's all part of it all. Whoever you are offering it to is part of it all, too. He who realizes that all of it is interrelated, all of it is one, becomes one with it all" (Ram Dass, p. 3).

    According to Judaism, in contrast, the *bracha* directs the mind and heart to the infinite source of the experience; however, we avoid suggestions that the Infinite has parts and in fact the unity of the Infinite is forever beyond our grasp. Rather, we acknowledge that the Infinite is the source of this finite experience. That knowledge, followed by sincere emotions of appreciation, can bring one to an extremely high level of *deveikus,* according to Ramban's definition (see end of Chapter 4).

15. Volozhin, R. Chaim, *Nefesh HaChaim,* "Eitz Chaim" 62. See also *ibid.* 1:13, where he identifies the mouth as the physiological locus of body-soul fusion. This view explains why we are built in a way that food enters and speech exits at the same locus: food because it maintains the fusion and speech because *brachos* maintain the soul's connection to the Infinite; without *brachos* we are cut off from the Source. Hence, proper use of the mouth is crucial to transcendence.

16. *Ibid.* 1:2–3.
17. *Talmud Sotah* 48b.
18. *Talmud Brachos* 33a.
19. Cf *Talmud Brachos* 60b.
20. Cf *Talmud Brachos* 54a.
21. Quoted in Pliskin, *Consulting the Wise,* p. 199.
22. *Talmud Menachos* 43b.
23. See R. Shneur Zalman, *Likutei Amarim Tanya,* "Shaar Hayichud," Chapter 2.

SIX

•

LOVE

The Art of Unity

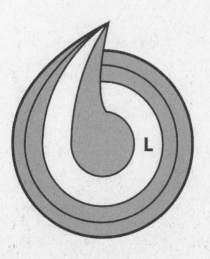

Become a Love Connoisseur

Mature Love

Level 1—Transcendental Love

Level 2—The Unity Meditation

Level 3—Meditation on Love

Level 4—The Day of Unity

Love, Intimacy, and Procreation

Even when one succeeds in enjoying aesthetic pleasure with total *kavana* and transcendental amazement, aesthetics cannot hold a candle to the pleasure of loving, caring relationships.

Yet how many people are searching for love but cannot define what it is they are looking for? What is love?

Intuitively, most people agree that love is higher than sensual pleasure in the sense that one would theoretically forego any sensory pleasures for the sake of love. Who would forsake true love for any amount of aesthetics?

For instance, imagine a stranger comes to your door with the following offer: "I'll give you fifty million dollars for your daughter. Nothing will happen to her. She'll just move to another country, and you'll never see or hear from her again. You won't even get a letter. You won't know a thing about her. But you'll get fifty million dollars." Who would seriously take it? Fifty million dollars (a mind-boggling amount of sensory pleasure) will not induce you to sell one child. There is no exchange rate; the pleasure of loving relationships is not negotiable for any amount of money.

Now, those parents who just turned down fifty million dollars for one of their children, what will they do when they walk back into their house and see their kid? They'll run over to her, hug and kiss her, tickle her, and say to themselves, "What is this creature who's worth more than all that money? Let's get to know this treasure that we have."

If the parents are working outside the home, they may realize that while they are practically killing themselves to earn money, they have a fortune at home worth more than they will ever earn, and they are not spending enough time with her. So moved, imagine they immediately decide to take that two-week vacation that the firm owes them, to spend time with their riches (i.e., children), and give the nanny a holiday.

The holiday begins fine. They take the kids to the park, read them a few stories, buy them a soda. . . . The first two hours, they're having a great time. But after a little while, things start to get tedious. The kids go from bickering to cranky to aggravating. Dinner was a disaster, giving them baths almost destroyed the hallway carpet, and bedtime seemed like War of the Worlds. Finally, at 10:00 P.M., the parents flop down on the couch, turn to each other, and say, "Do you really think it was the most responsible thing for us to have taken this two-week vacation? We're both so busy at work, maybe the right thing to do is to go back to work tomorrow morning."

What are these parents missing?

They are not connoisseurs. They never learned what love is and how to get the pleasure of loving relationships. You can tickle your kids only for so long. Just as for material pleasure we need a course in wine tasting, art appreciation, etc., to maximize our relationships, we need a course in human being "tasting," or appreciation.

BECOME A LOVE CONNOISSEUR

There are four points to becoming a connoisseur of love:

1: *Understand what love is.*

Love is the emotional pleasure that comes from recognizing someone's inner goodness. Everyone has some amount of goodness in them, but it is often challenging to focus on their goodness and not their faults. It is equally challenging to look beyond their surface appearance and recognize the personality inside. It is also difficult to focus on who they are rather than what they do for me.

To the extent that one can focus on virtues, one will love others—even if those others are throwing food at each other. One can love them and discipline them at the same time.

This definition of love accounts for how it is possible for people to "love" their cars or other objects. It simply requires focusing on the object's virtues. Since objects, unlike people, have no inner spiritual reality, such love is by comparison ridiculously shallow.

2: Out with the negative

Since the pleasure called love is a result of mental focus, it can be cultivated. As with many meditative practices, cultivating love requires first to clear the mind of negative thoughts and then to direct the mind toward the object of meditation.

The Torah in fact teaches exactly what kind of mental discipline or meditation is required to prepare us to love anyone.

Many religious groups consider the famous expression "Love your neighbor as yourself" a positive precept. But how could we be obliged to love? The beginning of the verse (Leviticus 19:18) may contain the key:

Don't take revenge; don't bear a grudge . . .
love your neighbor as yourself. . . .

In other words, by cessation of hostility and cleansing the mind of negative emotions toward someone, we can focus on their positive qualities.

This truth is demonstrable by its converse. Without understanding what love is and how to develop it, it is too easy to focus on the effort and pain involved in maintaining a relationship, such as marriage or raising children Sadly, many conclude that these pleasures are not worth the pain.

Every human being is a mixed bag of strengths and weaknesses. Focus on their virtues and you will come to love them; focus on their shortcomings and you will not want to spend five minutes with them. The effort of loving is not simply to find their virtues. The real effort is to make the commitment and take the responsibility to focus on their virtues and not their shortcomings.

3: Avoid "counterfeit" love.
While the soul seeks love, the body seeks love's counterfeit, infatuation or lust.

Today, infatuation often passes for love due to the influence of Hellenism, which has competed ideologically with Judaism for 2,300 years. Hellenism expresses its concept of love via the figure of Cupid in an effortless, magical, mystical happening: Two people are alone in Central Park, walking under the full moon and Cupid sneaks up behind them, while he's looking at her and she's looking at him. It shoots them both with an arrow, and they fall hopelessly in love. Effort-free loving!

However, just as easily as cupid-love comes, so it departs. Hollywood likes a happy ending, so we rarely see the long-term outcome of the romance. What ultimately happens to this couple in Central Park? The two of them fall in love and get married. Eventually they have kids, a big house, a heavy mortgage . . .

The husband has to work hard to pay the bills, so he stays overtime at the office. And late one night, while he's working with his secretary, Cupid sneaks up and shoots him again. Now he's in love with his secretary. He comes back to his wife and says, "What can I do, honey, that bum shot me again! I fell in love with the secretary." Out goes the wife—in comes the secretary. That's love, Greek style—not something you can choose but something that victimizes you, that you "fall into."

According to the Greeks, the only way to stay married is to hope Cupid will not shoot again.

Effort-free love is what we call infatuation. As with all material (M) pleasures, infatuation is ultimately not real because it is rooted in the body's desires and will ultimately disappear along with the body. Real love, as with all real pleasures, is forever.

The way to identify infatuation is simply to ask: does this feeling come from knowing his or her depth (a spiritual attraction), or does it come from looking at him or her (a physical attraction)? The mind must distinguish between messages from the soul and those from the body. Understand that real love takes real time and therefore real commitment. Infatuation is not love, only sensory attraction.

4: Accept the real price of love.

Imagine the following scene: The parents come home one day, gather their children around the dining room table and announce that they have fallen in love with the neighbors' children. "Please pack your belongings, as the other children will be moving in tomorrow." Could it happen?

While our children are accidents of birth, we choose our

spouse. Therefore, we should expect to see fewer breakups between spouses (or significant others) than between parents and children.

In fact, people rarely disown their children (as tempting as it may sometimes be) yet many divorce their spouses. Why is that? How come, given that spouses and children can equally aggravate us, we do not seriously think of disowning our kids?

Often when teaching about love, I will ask a visibly expectant mother if she will love the child. They always respond, "Of course."

"But," I protest, "how do you know your kid will not turn out to be a brat?"

They always reply, "I don't know, but I will love him or her anyway." Parents-to-be never say, "Well, we'll have the kid, get to know him, and we'll decide, based on his personality, if we want to keep him or not." How can they be so sure that they will love him?

People know that, as parents, they will be naturally committed to their offspring and appreciate their virtues. We do not fall out of love with anyone to whom we are committed. Thus, they can claim with confidence that they will love them, despite all shortcomings.

But love between consenting adults is not natural and only comes through effort.

The basic effort is to focus on virtue. Thus, the intensity of love is proportional to the extent to which one appreciates virtues.

But to know another's virtues in depth takes time, perhaps a lifetime. Therefore, the real price of love is long-term commitment. A short-term relationship will deliver relatively limited knowledge and therefore limited pleasure.

EXERCISES: *ARE YOU A CONNOISSEUR OF LOVE?*

How do you know if you are in love or infatuated?

If you ever catch yourself saying, "He [or she] is just perfect," beware! There is no such animal. That's a sure sign of infatuation, not love.

Make a mental list of five people whom you love. Ask yourself about each person: *Is s/he perfect?*

Real love takes work. If we want that pleasure, it's available within every relationship we have if we are willing to make the effort. Think of one person whom you would like to love with real love and commit to making the effort.

•

MATURE LOVE

The process of cultivating love leads naturally to a mature loving relationship, which is characterized by a feeling of oneness with an other.

We have all observed older couples who have been together for decades. Not only can they often complete each other's sentences, they even start to look alike. They are becoming one.

We learn this marriage ideal from the story of Adam and Eve. Genesis tells two contradictory versions of their creation:

VERSION 1 (1:27)
. . . male and female It created them.[1]

VERSION 2 (2:21–22)
. . . and It took one of his sides and closed the flesh in its place.
And . . . built the side that it took from the Adam into
a woman and brought her to the Adam.

What is the official story? Were Adam and Eve created simultaneously as the first version implies, or was Eve formed from Adam? According to the classical reconciliation of the two passages, the original Adam was a bi-gender being who was split into two halves. Not only does this interpretation underscore the inherent equality of men and women,[2] it supports the Kabbalistic teaching that before birth, a soul is split into two, one going into a woman's body and the other into a man's. When a couple find each other, the experience can literally be the joining of two halves into a new whole.[3]

This definition of love is alluded to in *gematria*. *Gematria* is the ancient system of assigning numerical values to words. It is based on the fact that Hebrew numbers are represented by letters: the first letter, aleph, equals 1; the second letter, beth/beis equals 2; and so on. Since every letter has a numerical value, every word can have a value as well, which is assigned according to the sum of its letters. According to the *gematria* tradition, two words with the same value must have some conceptual link. It is therefore instructive to note that the Hebrew words for love, *ahava*, and for oneness, *echad*, both have a numerical value of thirteen, hinting at an affiliation between the two.[4]

Now we can better understand a parent's natural love for his or her own children, even before birth. The child is quite literally an extension of the parent and the parent therefore feels a sense of unity with the child, regardless of the child's actions.

Similarly, this mature definition of love leads to a recipe for cultivating love: If I want to love someone, I only need to recognize and internalize what we have in common—our common humanity, our common history, our common culture, etc. My love for any person will grow the more that I can focus on their connection to me.

LEVEL 1—TRANSCENDENTAL LOVE

As with aesthetic pleasures, the pleasure of a loving relationship can become a transcendental experience with one additional *kavana:* amazement. When contemplating a loved one, one should not only enjoy the relationship, but also think, This person in my life is an amazing gift! Through that appreciative amazement, any loving relationship can theoretically become explosively transcendental. The key is to train ourselves to remember every day how everything—including this relationship—is a gift.

LEVEL 2—THE UNITY MEDITATION

Picture a typical old-fashioned map of the world: On the left is the Occident, including Africa and Western Europe—most of the world's Christians, pagans, and secular humanists. On the right is the Orient, with the major centers of Hinduism, Buddhism, and their derivatives.[5]

Near the center is Israel, the traditional frontier between East and West. Throughout history, great and small empires have coveted this tiny strip of land. Until the advent of modern transportation, it was a key trade route in the center of most of the world's population.

Israel also unites East and West in the area of meditative speech.

In the East and West alike, peoples have developed the use of speech as a spiritual practice, to direct the mind and heart.

The classical Western spiritual speech is prayer—to petition a god or "God." Whether formalized or improvised prayer, the typical Western way is to request fulfillment of needs and desires.

Eastern religion is stereotypically associated with a method of speech called the mantra. A mantra is a word or phrase repeated many times in order to center or guide the mind. One adopts a personal mantra and repeats it often throughout each meditation session and even throughout the day in order to unstick the mind from passing thoughts and desires and to guide it toward the desired spiritual goal of transcendence. The mantra is a useful, even powerful, tool to discipline the mind. But it is not a "prayer" in the Western sense.[6]

Jewish tradition falls near the middle of these two. From Abraham onward, Judaism has had both Western-style prayer and Eastern-style mantras. We see explicit examples in the Bible of Jews who pray in the traditional Western sense.[7] We also see examples in the Jewish mystical literature (*Kabbalah*) of the use of mantralike meditations. These two Jewish spiritual practices have been well documented elsewhere.[8]

What is less understood about Judaism is its middle path. The middle path is a meditative practice that was common to all Jews from Abraham until about 150 years ago, when the Jewish people began to fragment as never before. The relatively few who maintain this practice find it powerful enough to develop the most sublime *deveikus.*

To an observer, this type of meditation looks like our stereotype of prayer. In fact, Hebrew has no special word for prayer in the sense of "beseeching God." The closest word to prayer in the western sense of the word is *bakasha,* or "request."[9]

Indeed, this middle path has few peers east or west that can match its sublime beauty and raw power. It is called *Krias Sh'ma* (*Kriat Sh'ma*), or *Sh'ma* for short. Although it looks suspiciously like the familiar "Sh'ma Yisrael" that many Jews learn as children, by the end of this discussion it should look very different.

The Jewish Mission Statement

Every organization has a mission statement. Skillful managers know that the success of an organization largely depends on the degree to which its members have internalized the mission statement. Highly competitive organizations find creative ways to remind their members of the mission.

The *Sh'ma* meditation is the Jewish people's mission statement. It is written in the Torah[10] and is the simplest and purest amazement meditation of all time. This single phrase captures the essence of the classical Jew: a transcendental seeker, one who contemplates and struggles to grasp the Infinite, a witness to the essential unity of all things and a member of a tribe whose mission it is to preserve and perfect these modes of awareness.[11]

To use the *Sh'ma* properly requires a study of its nuances. The complete phrase is:

SH'MA YISRO'AYL
ADONOY ELOHAYNU
ADONOY ECHAD.

SH'MA—*hear,* as an imperative, meaning not just hearing but also deep understanding, at the gut level

YISRO'AYL—*Israel,* the Jewish people. The root means, "struggles with the Infinite"[12]

ADONOY—*the Infinite:* what was, is, and will ever be

ELOHAYNU—our power in the natural world[13]

ADONOY—*the Infinite:* what was, is, and will ever be

ECHAD—*one,* meaning absolute oneness, or perfect unity

Put together the meditation reads:

SH'MA YISRO 'AYL:
Understand—get into your gut—you who struggle with the Infinite:

ADONOY ELOHAYNU,

the Infinite (that which was, is, and will ever be) is our power in the natural world,

ADONOY ECHAD

the Infinite (that which was, is, and will ever be) is absolutely one.

•

How to Use It

There is a universal Jewish practice to say the *Sh'ma* meditation twice every day, morning and evening. This timing is derived from the Torah's phrase, to "speak these words ... when you go to bed and when you get up."[14]

Choose a place with minimal distractions. It may be a quiet room or location outside. Let the other members of your family know not to disturb you for five or ten minutes. If necessary, unplug the phone.

1. *Prepare the body:* wash your hands (review Chapter 4 for why and how). Assume the basic meditation position (see the end of Chapter 2).
2. *Prepare the mind:* if you are meditating in the morning, spend a few minutes thinking about light; if it is evening, spend a few moments thinking about the transition from day to night. In either case, follow with a few moments thinking about love.

3. *Cover the eyes* with the right hand. Think about your goal—a total understanding and internalization of the oneness of the Infinite.

4. *Say the six words of the* Sh'ma *phrase,* thinking about the meaning of each word as you say it. Say the words aloud. Hear your voice intone them.

5. *Repeat* as many times as you need. The goal is to say the entire phrase at least once with 100 percent *kavana*.[15] If you realize, for instance, that upon saying "echad" you did not have kavana on the word "Yisrael," say the whole thing again. When you arrive to the "d" of "echad" and feel a total concentrated transcendence, stop repeating the phrase.

6. *Warm-down:* bring yourself back gently to space-time by whispering the mystical tagline:

BARUCH SHAYM KAVOD MAL-CHUSO
LAY-OLAM VAH-ED.
The revelation of the awesomeness of the Infinite's omnipresent
and omnipotent manifestation is the source of blessing
for the eternal hidden world.[16]

That's a real mouthful in English and requires an explanation.

The word *shaym* in the vernacular means "name," and in the mystical language of classical Hebrew the name of a person or thing reveals that person or thing's essence.

Therefore, the *Baruch shaym* tagline literally refers to the Infinite's four-letter name, spelled *yud* + *hay* + *vav* + *hay*.

This name expresses as much of the Infinite's revealed or manifest essence as classical Hebrew can (some would say, as much as possible in this world).

Consequently, this four-letter name is awesome, and a spiritual seeker should approach it with real humility. Consequently, we have a universal custom not to pronounce it as written. Instead, we pronounce it "Adonoy," having in mind "the Infinite,"—i.e., that which was, is, and will always be.

This pronunciation, Adonoy, also has the connotation of "master of the universe," which indicates one aspect of our relationship to the Infinite.

Some people have tried to pronounce the four-letter name as written.[17] This practice can generate dreadful karma[18] and is not advised, for to do so is akin to flippancy about the manifest essence of the Infinite.

The universal Jewish practice today is to be so sensitive to the karma connected with this name that in casual speech we are taught to avoid even pronouncing the ersatz name *Adonoy,* substituting instead "Ha-*shem*"—literally, "the name."

Now, by definition the Infinite must be totally manifest in the finite—it's *everywhere, all the time!* In times of need, many people, regardless of religious background, do express some transcendental awareness through prayer and/or meditation. Nevertheless, in ordinary times, most people remain ensconced in nature and naturalism, ignoring the concept of an omnipresent and omnipotent Infinite.

Key to Kavana

Before saying the *Sh'ma,*

remember that millions of Jews

say this mission statement

every day, as we have for

thousands of years.

This fact of human nature is why in the *Sh'ma* we say *"Elo-heinu"*—"our" power in nature. From the dawn of Jewish history until today, this knowledge has yet to become universal.

Yet our own knowledge is limited. From the greatest to the smallest, we are all mere seekers of spiritual understanding. True, we may develop our awareness of the Infinite's manifestation in the finite world—this is the goal of Judaism's meditative practices. This awareness is awesome—*amazing!* The fact that we can express this awareness is more amazing still.

But there are even greater dimensions of amazement.

In seeking Infinite awareness, Jewish tradition often represents the Infinite with the metaphor of a king and its manifestation with a kingdom. According to this metaphor, human beings have a greater role than passive recipients of Infinite pleasure. A "king" cannot "rule" without "subjects." If there were not humans actively to "make the Infinite king" so to speak, then It could not be King. It could not have a meaningful or relevant relationship to the finite.

In other words, by choosing to receive, we *make it possible* for the Infinite to give.

This is an amazing insight and an awesome responsibility, which leads to several startling conclusions.

Consider, for instance, the *bracha* meditation of Chapter 5. At the basic level, the purpose of the *bracha* is to expand a great aesthetic pleasure, such as eating a piece of fruit, into a transcendental pleasure.

But we can now see that something else is happening when we say a *bracha* with *kavana*.

Recall that the purpose of this universe is for our total pleasure, the greatest of which would be infinite, transcendental pleasure. In other words, our purpose is to elevate the physical and to make our interaction with it and our experience of it transcendental. That is, to reveal the Infinite's manifestation.

Therefore, if human beings ceased to use the physical for ultimate (transcendental) pleasure, there would be no ultimate purpose for the existence of that physical pleasure. The Infinite would cease to make that physical pleasure manifest. In other words, if people stopped making *brachos* on oranges, oranges would stop growing.[19]

This awesome responsibility is taught many places in Jewish tradition, the first of which is the Torah's account of Adam, the first Homo sapiens with an Infinite soul:

> All the trees of the field were not yet on the earth and all the plant-life of the field not yet sprouted, for the Infinite-Manifest had not caused rain to fall and there was no Adam to work the ground.
>
> GENESIS 2:5

The Midrash explains that the rain started to fall as soon as Adam asked for it.[20] Now, as Chapter 7 will explain, the Torah is not a history book; we are meant to ask what this passage can *teach* us. To which one might answer that the basic lesson is the interdependent relationship between physical blessings and ourselves. Not only do we depend on blessings, the blessings depend on us.

> The bracha *thus creates a new reality—one in which the blessings from the Infinite Source may descend upon the one who has uttered the* bracha.
>
> RABBI AARON TWERSKI[21]

We are in fact describing Jewish "karma," mentioned in previous chapters. The basic principle of karma is that our words and actions in this world have both material and spiritual effects. When enjoying the material world, since we already have the experience in our hand (in the case of food, literally in our hand), we cannot say that this current experience depends on the utterance of a *bracha.* The reason is simply because it is clearly possible to have the experience without a *bracha.* Therefore, if the *bracha* does have a karmic effect, that effect must be on future experiences.

Our words, then, can have tremendous power.

This potential of our own words helps clarify the discussion above, regarding the indirect way we pronounce the four-letter name. We do not avoid the name altogether. In a *bracha,* as well as in the *Sh'ma,* we do meditate on the name, using the pronunciation *Adonoy.* With deep *kavana,* these meditations can feel pretty good. In fact, when one says the six-word *Sh'ma* meditation with *kavana,* it can feel as though one has grasped the essence of the Infinite.

This feeling jibes well with the transcendental reality of the Infinite. The transcendental reality should be stop-you-in-your-tracks-speechless, jaw-droppingly-awe-inspiring. The four-letter name, which expresses that reality, should likewise be awesome.

This name has such power that Jewish practice strictly limits pronouncing it to once per year by the High Priest in the Jerusalem Temple, to be heard by the assembled public. He utters it after many hours of intense physical and mental preparation and purification on Yom Kippur, the day the entire nation have most intensified their physical and mental purification.

This tradition teaches us a lesson in humility. One should think, How can I even momentarily think that I truly grasp the Infinite's essence?

Therefore, to hedge our *kavana*, the *Baruch shaym* tagline reminds us that we really cannot properly relate to the name that we are trying to say.

The tag solves the dilemma of the *Sh'ma* meditation: when said with *kavana*, one can have the feeling of actually grasping the essence of the name. The tag brings us back down to earth. It reminds us that the energy associated with the name is really beyond our grasp.

Please review the tagline and its translation, above. Then try the exercises below.

EXERCISE

1. Try the first-level *Sh'ma* meditation. Do it for a week, either every morning or every evening, or both morning and evening.

2. After doing the *Sh'ma* meditation for at least a week, make a commitment to yourself to continue daily for three more weeks.

3. After doing the *Sh'ma* meditation for a week or two, continue with level three, below.

LEVEL 3—MEDITATION ON LOVE

By itself, the first line of the *Sh'ma* is a meditation of awesome power. We can harness that power to tap into the deepest, most beautiful human emotions. While everyone has the capacity for these emotions, they do not always come naturally.

It has been observed that the degree to which we feel fondness for someone or something is directly proportional to the amount of time involved. We tend to develop fondness for those with whom we spend the most time.

This model gives us an alternative explanation as to why people can "love" their cars. The typical car lover does not spend time with his car only because he loves it; he loves it more because he spends time with it!

In other words, love can be cultivated. Contrary to popular belief (and song), love need not be spontaneous. Most of what people experience as "love at first sight" is probably infatuation or lust—i.e., self-centered desire. After all, how could it be true love? By definition, true love develops from an appreciation of another person's virtues. This appreciation may take weeks, months, or even years. But a true lover is like a true painter: he will take as much time as needed. For love is indeed an art form—a sophisticated craft that demands creative brilliance and hard work.

Now, when we say the short *Sh'ma* meditation properly, we find that doorways open within ourselves, doorways which lead to our own infinite qualities. The general name for this range of qualities is love. Love is the best word we have for that aspect of a human being that is most akin to the Infinite. This point is symbolized by the Hebrew words for love, *ahava*, and for oneness, *echad*. Both words have a numerical value of 13, hinting at an affiliation between the two. Combined, 13+13 = 26, which is the numerical value for Infinite's unspeakable name, Y-H-V-H.

Moreover, the three-letter root of *ahava* (AHB) has the numerical value of eight. In Kabbalah, eight represents infinity, which is appropriately symbolized by our modern numeral, 8 (turn it sideways).

Therefore, since the gates are open, the logical continuation of the short *Sh'ma* would be a deeper meditation on infinite love. When we say the *Sh'ma* well, we should feel so connected that we want to connect. It feels good. We feel a powerful urge to connect to that source of light and love. Our instinctive response is to want more light and love.[22]

This is indeed the next step—in fact, the Torah itself teaches a deep meditation on love immediately after the first line of the *Sh'ma* meditation. Why love? Again: because that is what we should be feeling after saying the *Sh'ma*. To say the love paragraph with *kavana* will help us meditate with more *kavana* in the future, which in turn helps us develop more love . . . and so on.

EXERCISE

1. Compare and contrast: prayer, mantra, *Sh'ma.*

2. After taking the time to learn the *Sh'ma* meditation with proper *kavana,* begin to use the second paragraph. Start by reading the translation carefully. As always, make sure that you have crystal clarity each step of the journey.

Follow the same technique outlined above. For the sake of maximum accuracy in pronunciation, follow the transliteration with care. The consonant "ch" represents the guttural that is often transliterated as "ch" and sounds like someone clearing their throat.[23]

•

(with eyes closed, aloud:)

SH'MA YISRO'AYL Understand—get into your gut—
you who struggle with the Infinite

ADONOY ELOHAYNU the Infinite (that which was, is,
and will ever be) is our power in nature;

ADONOY ECHAD the Infinite (that which was, is, and
will ever be) is absolutely one.

(whispered:)

BARUCH SHAYM KAVOD MAL-CHUSO LAY-OLAM VAH-ED.
The revelation of the awesomeness of the Infinite's
omnipresent and omnipotent manifestation is the
source of blessing for the eternal hidden world.

Vay'ahav-TAW es ADONOI ello-heh-chaw,
Love the Infinite, your power in nature,

bchol l'vah-ve-CHAW,
with a full-heart (i.e., both spiritual
and material drives),

uveh-chol naf-sheh-CHAW,
with your entire soul (willing to die for
transcendental pleasure),

uveh-chol m'o-DEH-chaw.
and with all your resources (willing even to spend
money for transcendence).

V'hah-yu,
And they will be,

hah-d'vareem ha-ayleh ashayr ah-nochi
*m'tsa-v'*CHAW *ha-yohm,*
these words with which I give you
transcendental access today,

*ahl l'*VA-VEH-*chaw.*
upon your heart (internalized into both spiritual
and material drives).

*V'shee-nahn-*TAHM *l'vah-neh-chaw,*
*v'deebar*TA *bahm*
And you will imbue your children with them,
and meditate with them

b'shiv-t'cha b'vay-seh-chaw, uvehlech-teh-chaw
va-derech,
both sitting at home and traveling on the road,

*uv'shach-beh-chaw uvehku-*MEH-*chaw.*
both in the evening and in the morning.

*Ukih-shar*TAM *l'os al yah-deh-chaw,*
And you'll bind them as a symbol of physical
discipline to your arm,

veh-hayu l'totafos bayn ay-neh-chaw.
and they'll be a sign of mental discipline
between your eyes.

Uk'sav-TAM al m'zuzos bay-SEH-chaw,
And you'll write them on the doorposts
of your house,

uvee-shar-ehcha.
and on your gates.

Discussion

The theme of the meditation is the constant awareness of the Infinite throughout one's daily life, as you practiced in Chapter 4. A person who is aware and observant is sometimes called an *ayd,* a witness. The first line is written as a testimonial: *Hear and understand . . . !* As a postmodern twist to an ancient text, in every Torah scroll in the world, from Yemen to San Francisco, two letters in this phrase are written much larger than the rest of the line. These two letters, *ayin* and *daled,* spell *ayd*—witness.

The long paragraph above continues this theme of awareness, taking us from pure transcendental awareness through some of the details of the love created through that intimate awareness.

LEVEL 4—THE DAY OF UNITY

The *Sh'ma* meditation, and particularly the first six words, is a tool to refocus on the true transcendental potential of the world. Paradoxically, in order to tune in to this reality, we tune out certain aspects of the world. For a moment, we tune out life's pressing details. Hunger, work, family, friends, war, peace, telephones, music and television, machines, pencils, dirty laundry, money—all become irrelevant for a moment while we reconnect to something much more lasting and satisfying.

Who would not benefit from a daily five-minute meditation like this?

But imagine taking the time every week to live an *entire day* with oneness, literally to turn off and put aside those activities that keep us attached to the mundane side of this world: telephones, music and television, machines, pencils, dirty laundry, money, work—a whole day of *Sh'ma*—of hearing! A day of outward focus, of human relationships without the pressure to accomplish or to produce; and a day of inward meditation, to reconnect to ourselves and to something greater. This incredible idea is itself worth the price of this book: to spend twenty-four hours seeking "infinity in a grain of sand, heaven in a wild flower" (William Blake). A single day spent without seeking to manipulate, only to enjoy life at every level.

Now, imagine an entire community practicing such a day of meditation. Again, it is instructive to see Israel's synthesis of East and West.

In the stereotypical East, we see cultures dominated by communal focus. The welfare of the community takes precedence over the ambitions of the individual. Social norms are dominant and stable.

In the stereotypical West, we see cultures dominated by

the individual focus. The rights of the individual take priority over the cohesion of the community. Social norms are fluid and routinely violated, even overturned.

The Jewish ideal balances between the community and the individual by shifting the concept of individual rights to individual responsibilities. It is a subtle shift that can transform the social relationships that are the foundation of the community.

For instance, imagine a society where, instead of the needy competing for limited social welfare, we had many people competing to help the impoverished. If everyone considered it a sacred responsibility to give 10 percent of their income to the poor, it would become increasingly difficult to find poverty.

Under this ideal, the dominant, inviolate social norm is to give to others. The individual freedom is the freedom to choose whether or not to give and how and when to give.

Internalizing this sense of responsibility—balancing East and West—is the key to loving relationships. To cultivate a culture of such loving responsibility seems, historically, to require a day when economic and social competition ceases and individuals can focus exclusively on their individual meditations and social relationships.

To *be* for a day—to "stop" changing the world—is the meaning of Shabbat, a weekly rhythmic interlude of spiritual rest, meditative contemplation, and community building.[24]

Although many find this model attractive, they rationalize, "Maybe I'll try it when I have time. . . ." *Perhaps you'll never have time?*[25]

LOVE, INTIMACY, AND PROCREATION

The stronger the potential love bond, the stronger the potential material quagmire. Marriage has fantastic love potential, which is why the sex drive is so strong. When practiced outside of a committed, lifelong relationship, one risks feeding their bodily desire for sex at the expense of the soul's desire for love. Alternatively, in the context of love (i.e., unity), intimate relations have the power to make that unity love indescribably profound.[26]

The two challenges of loving relationships should now be evident: how to enjoy them and how to use them as vehicles for amazing spiritual transcendence. The exercises should lead toward a love experience so profound that it is hard to imagine a greater pleasure.

NOTES

1. Traditional translations render the Hebrew *hu* as "He"; however, the same pronoun also denotes "It." In order to avoid the common error of personifying the Infinite Creator as a man, I have used the neutral pronoun.
2. Cf Hirsch, *Commentary on the Torah,* on this verse.
3. Cf Rashi on this verse, who observes that a child is literally a new whole produced from equal halves of the parents.
4. See *Kli Yakar* on Genesis 2:5, reference "Bayom."

5. I am not "conveniently" forgetting the Americas. The map represents the civilized world during the formative era of the great religions—i.e., until the Middle Ages.

6. *Talmud Brachos* 31a. See Rashi there who defines tefila, as "praise." See also the Introduction to Rabbi Shimshon Pincus's classic, *Shaarim B'Tefila*. See also *ibid.* p. 93. Some people equate all forms of meditative speech, e.g., Stephen Levine, *A Gradual Awakening*: "A basic difference between various meditation forms—such as TM, or Sufi dancing, or confronting Zen koans, or sitting meditations, or Christian prayer, or chanting mantra, or listening to the inner sound current, or cycling light, or observing sensations in the body, or visualizing techniques, or watching the breath—is the primary object on which concentration is developed" (p. 2). This blurs an important distinction. While prayer is indeed a form of meditation, its goal is not concentration per se. Similar differences arise when we contrast Sufi dancing and Zen koans, two of Levine's examples.

7. E.g., Genesis 20:17, 25:21, 32:10–13, Exodus 32:11.

8. See Kaplan, *Meditation and the Bible;* also *Meditation and Kabbalah.*

9. Cf Rashi on Numbers 31:8, where he distinguishes between *tefila* and *bakasha.*

10. *Deuteronomy* 6:4.

11. See *MB* 62:3, which summarizes the *kavana* of the *Sh'ma* as IKUVA—"essentiality."

12. There are various opinions on what the word Yisrael means. The verse (Genesis 32:29) says: "Your name will no longer be said as Yaakov rather Yisroel because you have *sarisa* with God and with men and done well." The word sarisa may mean "excelled," "been straight" (as opposed to the "crooked" nature of a "Yaakov" which means bent) or "struggled." Since the context is an all-night wrestling match many prefer the latter.

See Rashi and Radak (R. David Kimchi) there. Both cite Hosea 12:4–5. Hizkuni sees Yaakov as having equaled—but not bested—the angel of God. R. Hirsch (*op. cit.*) points out that, grammatically, *sarisa* means "you had power"; thus, homiletically, if a lowly person like Yaakov can prevail, then there must be a higher power making it so.

13. See Rashi on Genesis 2:5.

14. Deuteronomy 6:7.

15. *MT Book of Love,* Ways of Krias Sh'ma 2:1; *Shulchan Aruch Orach Chaim* 63:4 and *Mishna Berura* there 12–15. See also Taz on *Shulchan Aruch Orach Chaim* 61:9. However, one should strive to say it right the first time.

16. Cf Hirsch., *et al.* commentaries on Deuteronomy 6:4.

17. For the sake of clarity, here are the two most prevalent examples of this practice; however, the reader is discouraged from pronouncing them aloud: Jehovah, Yahweh.

18. *Talmud Nedarim* 7b.

19. See Tosafos on *Talmud Brachos* 43a.

20. *Y. Taanis* 2: the word *ayd* ("mist") in verse 6 can be read as "prayer." See Rashi on Genesis 2:5, where he paraphrases *Talmud Hulin* 60b.

21. "100 Times a Day," in Forst, Rabbi Binyamin, *The Laws of B'rachos,* New York, Mesorah, 1990, p. 29.

22. Refined feelings are the result of spiritual work, but not the work itself. Despite our desire for immediate emotional gratification, the mind should lead the heart and not vice versa. As we improve our understanding of life and of ourselves, our emotions mature naturally (Velozhin, *Nefesh HaChaim,* Ch. 13).

23. The translation follows the exegesis of several authorities, including Rashi, Rambam, and Ramban. See Deuteronomy 6:4-9.

24. See Mozeson, p. 169.

25. *Talmud Avos* 2:17.

26. Heterosexual intimacy in particular has the potential for transcendental pleasure in a dimension much greater than other physical experiences. This is for two reasons. First, the mystical tradition interprets the intimacy between a man and a woman as an analogy to that between the Infinite and the Finite. Second, the creation of a child—a new living creature—is the most "Divine" creative activity available to us.

This framework is not to negate the possibility of loving intimacy without the potential for procreation. Rather, the point is that the potential for procreation—even the imitation of the potential—adds a transcendental dimension to the intimacy, when practiced with *kavana*.

SEVEN

•

BEING GOOD

The Art of Not Caring
What They Think

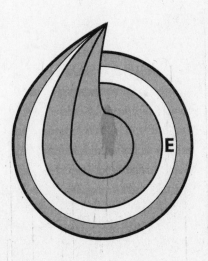

Everyone wants to do what is right. According to a *U.S. News & World Report* poll, nine of ten Americans say that they consider themselves good people. Are they right? On what basis do they say so?

According to the poll, this 90 percent judge themselves more favorably than they judge Mother Teresa (80 percent) and Michael Jordan (70 percent). The fact that most people judge themselves so favorably indicates a deep psychological phenomenon: Being ethical is so important that few can bear the possibility of being unethical.

Not only do we consider ourselves "basically good," but we even tend to think of ourselves as "better than most." In fact, according to the *U.S. News* poll, most of us consider ourselves saintly. Yet somehow we bristle at the idea that even Hitler in his own warped way believed he was righteous. If Hitler could be so evil yet consider himself good, what about we who are so . . . ? No, file the Hitlers of the world under the category of "crazy" rather than use these examples as an opportunity to introspect and to evaluate our own righteousness.

I'm a moral person but I think, like most people,
my moral values are pretty fuzzy.
MICK JAGGER

A DEFINITION

Good or *ethical* means acting in accordance with an absolute value. For example, in every society most people believe that to murder is wrong or evil and not to murder is good; that robbery is evil and that honesty is good; etc.

If so, why do so many people commit murder, rob, lie, cheat, and so on? There are two underlying reasons.

One reason is multiple definitions of what, exactly, constitutes murder, robbery, etc. Some would say the evil of murder includes the killing of animals. Some say the termination of a pregnancy is murder. Others disagree.

A second reason for the prevalence of these evils is that people tend to rationalize: "I know this is wrong, but . . ." Or: "I know his behavior is bad, but he has a good heart." Normal people simply do not knowingly and intentionally commit or abet evil.

In fact, our aversion to evil is so strong that in order to avoid it, we would be willing to sacrifice not only physical pleasures but even loved ones—even life itself.

For instance, imagine you were on a plane hijacked by terrorists. They come up to you and say, "Either you kill these three hundred innocent people on the plane—here's the gun, go and slaughter them—or we'll kill your kids."

What would you do? Could you kill three hundred innocent people? You couldn't do it. Even though you have five kids you adore, you still could not kill three hundred innocent people. Why not? Because it's wrong.

The devil's advocate asks, "But wait a minute. Are you some angel? Didn't you ever do anything wrong in your life? What's the big deal? Do one more wrong thing."

"No. It's *too* wrong. It's not worth it."

"What's not worth what?"

"The pleasure of my loving relationships is not worth giving up the pleasure of being good."

Do you realize what you are saying? You are willing to give up your most cherished loving relationships in order to avoid evil and to be ethical. Goodness is a greater or higher type of pleasure.

If the example of the three hundred innocent lives doesn't resonate, choose a higher number—three thousand or even three million. At some point, every sane person draws the line and says that they would rather give up a loved one than commit evil.

Now if the pleasure of being good outweighs much of what we have in life, we should learn how to enjoy that pleasure.

In other words—Judaism teaches—if you do not know

what you're willing to die for, you have not begun to live. If you have no self-respect, no belief that you yourself are a good person, you are not yet living life to the fullest.

The drive for self-respect is so strong that most people consider themselves good even if they have never examined what it means to be good.

Contrast this unawareness with our attitude toward the pleasures discussed in previous chapters. People don't mind admitting their lack of physical pleasure. We readily and openly discuss our search for loving relationships (and the transparency of these two unmet needs drives major sectors of our economy). Yet where are all the seekers of righteousness?

Part of the problem is a culture that has drummed into us a notion of tolerance so broad as to accept all perspectives and lifestyles as equally good. Perhaps 9/11 has helped clarify in our hearts that there are indeed some beliefs and actions that are evil.

THE DIFFERENCE BETWEEN RIGHT AND WRONG

How can we define the absolute values that determine whether actions are right or wrong?

Although I know there are a lot of gray areas, I used to take comfort in knowing that there were certain deeds that were universally accepted as good or bad. For instance, everyone in every land agreed that it would be good to save a small child's life and wrong to murder.

Then came 9/11.

At 9/11 we learned about a group of people who not out of anger or despair but for rational, thoughtful reasons concluded that it would be good to murder thousands of people.

They don't even call it murder.

How do we know we're right and they are wrong? How does one iconoclast like Abraham know that it is possible to be right "even if the rest of the world says you're wrong"?[1]

First, we know that whatever sense of "absolute right and wrong" we have is something we believe irrationally. Even the Declaration of Independence resorted "self-evident" truths. The deepest truths cannot be proven, they can only be revealed.

It is likely that every sane human being on earth agrees that killing an innocent person is murder. The disagreements stem from how to define human—for instance, Nazis and jihad-ists may define *person* as "non-Jewish." Others may define *human* as "white."

When confronted with this apparent chaos of values, Jewish tradition reminds us that our perception of events in this world is fundamentally illusory. There really is only one absolute, true reality—the infinite Source of existence. Thus, *good* is defined simply as a belief or activity that interfaces with or is consistent with that Source, whereas *bad* is a belief or activity that does not interface with or is inconsistent with that Source.

Even more simply put, good is that which draws me closer to that Source (creating greater *deveikus*) and bad (or evil) is that which draws me away from the Source.

This streamlined definition of good does not fully resolve the problem. It still leaves room for interpretation of what kinds of beliefs and activities draw one closer to the Source. Some would claim that the answer is completely subjective. The problem with such a view is that there are some beliefs and activities that most of us label bad without hesitation.

For example, a Taliban may claim that flying an airplane into a building full of civilians would bring them closer and faster to the Source. Most non-Taliban disagree: It is not merely a subjective choice. Prior to 9/11, such an example would have seemed grossly exaggerated and inappropriate. Unfortunately, our collective karma is forcing us more and more to confront these ethical questions and refine our own moral principles.

But the struggle is just as real on the individual level. If I am feeling grumpy, is it "wrong" to act grumpily toward my spouse? Perhaps for the sake of honesty, acting grumpy would be right.

Without a framework, it is impossible to answer such a question with any ethical certainty. What we gain from the Jewish definition of good is the ability to say that certain actions (and beliefs) are objectively good and others are objectively bad. How objectively to differentiate remains to be seen.

MORALITY AS A BODY-SOUL STRUGGLE

Let us consider a person with enough moral clarity to know without any doubt that stealing is wrong—evil, in fact. What might lead such a person to steal?

Consider the scenario of a vice president of a company who has made a mistake that will cost the company thousands of dollars. The only other person who knows about the mistake is a secretary. What should the manager do—blame and fire the secretary ("It's my word against hers") or . . . admit the mistake: to say, effectively, "I'm wrong."

What would motivate an otherwise decent person to blame the secretary? Whether or not telling the truth will result in material consequences, most people have a hard time admitting their mistakes from fear of looking bad. Looking bad—a painful experience for the body—is a powerful disincentive to honesty.

Yet time and again we hear of people who confess their mistakes, sometimes many years later. For many years they choose to look good rather than to be good—following the body rather than the soul. Yet all along, the soul clamors for the pleasure of being good, the pleasure of self-respect.

HOW TO LEARN HOW TO BE GOOD

As a child grows, she slowly learns to identify the different forces within her. One voice says, "Hit your brother." The other voice says, "Leave him alone."

If good refers to actions that draw her closer to the Infinite source and bad to those that draw her away, then she can interpret the two voices within the context of the body-soul struggle that makes our spiritual growth possible.

Thus, the first voice ("hit your brother") is her body (material self) and the other voice ("leave him alone") is her soul (spiritual self).

In real-life situations, it is easy to tell the difference.

Whenever you are contemplating doing something and are not sure if it would be right or wrong, ask yourself the following questions:

What do I *feel* like doing?
What do I *know* is the right thing to do?

In an ethical decision, *what I feel like doing* is always the body talking and *what I know is the right thing to do* is always the soul talking.

EXERCISE—*IDENTIFY YOUR ETHICAL CHOICES*

To appreciate the pleasure of our own goodness is a level of amazement. In order to develop this appreciation, make a list of ethical choices you have faced today (whether or not you chose well). This is the first step to becoming a connoisseur of anything—learning to discriminate between different qualities.

Place a check mark beside those choices in which you chose to do what you believe is right and an *X* beside those in which you chose to do what you felt like doing.

Make such a list every evening for one week. The goal is to develop awareness of ethical choices as we are making them.

•

As a person grows morally, one trains the body (feelings) to conform to the soul (knowledge) so that one's gut reaction becomes more and more consistent with the spiritual or good path. The synchronization of body with soul is what we call maturity.

One might suppose that highly mature individuals get

their bodies so in tune with their souls that they eventually run out of moral choices.

This might be true if the soul were finite. But since the soul is rooted in an infinite source, spiritual growth too is infinite. A spiritually mature person indeed faces daily moral choices. The difference between a spiritually immature person and a spiritually mature person is the level of refinement of those choices.

For instance, most of us at least occasionally struggle to control our impatience with certain people. Every workplace has at least one of them: the obnoxious guy, the rude woman, the conceited person. A highly spiritual individual will not struggle with whether or not to show any kindness to such a person, but may struggle with whether or not to give that person an extra few minutes of kindliness.

Our history is resplendent with spiritual giants who lived up to such standards. Open any biography of any Jewish sage and one finds story after story of great kindness and generosity extended under the most trying circumstances—circumstances that the average person would not have tolerated. The basic generosity is not an issue for such great people—this is part of their nature. Their moral struggles are in minute details that would be irrelevant to the rest of us.

To give but one example: Rabbi Moshe Feinstein, one of the greatest of twentieth century sages, always attracted a crowd when he went outside his home in New York. Once, a particularly eager student rushed to help the Rav get into his car, and in doing so, slammed the door shut on Rav Moshe's finger. Yet the Rav did not cry out—indeed, he did not react at all and the other occupants of the car did not realize what had happened until the car had driven several blocks and Rav Moshe opened the door to relieve his finger.

While a doctor treated the wound, an astonished student asked how it could be that Rav Moshe uttered no expression of pain when the door was closed on his hand. Rav Moshe was reportedly taken aback with the question: "What? And embarrass that young man in public? God forbid!"

Most of us would have struggled not to swear or shout epithets at the offending student. Rav Moshe's level of self-control was considerably more refined.

YOU'RE SO BAD? HOW TO BECOME GOOD AGAIN

Faced with so many daily body-soul struggles, we inevitably make the wrong choice once in awhile. Sometimes my mistakes hurt me and myself alone and at other times they hurt others.

In all cases, my decision to listen to my body instead of my soul—in other words, to choose wrongly—leaves me in a state of "wrongness." I am now a "wrong" or "bad" person, according to the magnitude of the deed.

The way to correct the situation and make myself right and "good" again is to restore the situation to its pre-mistake balance.

If, for instance, my mistake was to eat a meal like an animal and not like a connoisseur, I can correct the situation by internalizing the meaning of what I have done and committing myself to make the right choice in the future.

Of course, the only way I can know for sure that I have fully corrected the mistake is when I find myself in exactly the same situation again with the same bodily, material temptation and choose to listen to my soul this time around.

If I make a mistake in my treatment of another person, I must also make full amends to the person. If, for instance, I stole something from them, I must return the item or its value. But paying them back materially only restores the material balance to the relationship. Chances are my bad choice caused emotional damage as well. The only way to restore the emotional balance is to receive forgiveness.

Practical Application of This Model of Goodness

From this framework Jewish tradition draws powerful practical suggestions.

First, because of our near enslavement to our bodies, we find it excruciatingly difficult to say two particular two-word phrases: "I'm wrong" and "I'm sorry." The reason we find these two phrases so difficult is because we live in a society that does not acknowledge the body-soul duality. Society says, "You are a body" and therefore it is very important that your body be beautiful—looking good.

Alternatively, a person who recognizes that the body

houses a soul that is the true self will focus on making the soul beautiful, even at the expense of the body's appearance to others—being good.

Therefore, in order to be a good person, one absolutely must master the art of saying "I'm wrong" and "I'm sorry." Unless one is flawless, it is impossible to sustain a relationship with anyone without making occasional wrong choices that hurt the other person. The pain causes strain but many distressed relationships can be turned around by both parties simply learning how to say these two phrases with conviction.

A person who does not know what is genuine goodness will likely expend a lot of effort trying to win the admiration of others in order to make himself feel important. We call this counterfeit pleasure "being a success." Too often in our society, you can be a good wife or husband, a good friend, a loyal human being, but if you are not "successful" you are a failure. Even though on some level everybody knows that people can appear very successful and still be the dregs of society, most Americans believe that if you do not appear successful, you have not made it in life.

Do not fall for "looking" good. Self-respect is the genuine pleasure. It is a basic energy we all need. Without self-respect, something central about our humanity is missing. Everyone needs to feel their life has some lasting value. Even though a person may have awesome material pleasure—vacations, a dream home, designer clothing—and even enviable emotional pleasure—a wonderful soul mate, great friends, and children—these pleasures do not themselves prevent that moment of crisis when we say "So what! What has it all led up to? What have I done of lasting value?" To really live, we need to tap into the pleasure of being good.

One of the best ways to cultivate goodness is to reflect at the end of each day or week, once the pain of carrying out responsibilities is gone (as per the previous exercise). The next step is to look back and appreciate the meaning of living a good life and to take pleasure in the specific goodness that one has accomplished over a longer time frame.

EXERCISES: *BECOME A CONNOISSEUR OF BEING GOOD*

Make a list of twenty things you did during the past ten years that gave you a sense of accomplishment. Check those that were real pleasures (being good) and an *X* next to counterfeit pleasures (looking good).

Find a time once a week to reflect upon the week's meaningful accomplishments. Identify how each moral choice was an opportunity to become a better person.

•

GOOD ISN'T GOOD ENOUGH:
THE PATH TO GREATNESS

While goodness is measured in terms of an absolute, no human being can be absolutely good. This is because the absolute yardstick we use to measure our goodness is the infinite source of life—there is infinite potential for growth. One might even trick one's body that works against spiritual growth by saying that, given that I am already good (a concession to my vanity), I can nonetheless desire and strive to be *great*.

In order to become systematically a better person requires a discipline of introspection. We have a form of introspection-meditation used by some of the great Jewish mystics. To enable deep introspection, they would isolate themselves from others. The Ba'al Shem Tov (the founder of modern Hasidism) used to seek solitude in the Russian forest.

Modern psychology has tapped into this principle with the isolation tank. An isolation tank is a pool of water that is exactly body temperature and exactly body density, which means you float in it effortlessly like in the Dead Sea, and you feel no sensation in your skin because it's your temperature. The room is absolutely dark and there is no sound. So what do you have left after you've taken away physical sensation and sound and light? You are left with your thoughts.

We call meditation of introspection *hisbodedus (hitbodedut)*, which literally means "isolation." Practically speaking, introspection is indeed most effective in isolation—away from interruptions and other distractions. Of course, isolation tanks and forests are not required. One can introspect in any suitable place of isolation.

Nor does one need to devote long periods of time to *hisbodedus*. While some Hasidic masters recommend up to an hour a day, the average person will benefit from even a few daily minutes.

It is crucial, however, that those five or so minutes be uninterrupted. It is also very helpful that one's daily *hisbodedus* be at the same time and location.

Spend those five minutes asking and answering one or more deeply personal questions. Rabbi Aryeh Kaplan suggests the following as examples:

- *What do I want out of life?*
- *What gives my life meaning?*
- *What is the purpose/meaning of life in general?*
- *If I could redo my life until now, what would I change?*
- *What would I be willing to die for?*
- *What would bring me more happiness than anything else in the world?*[2]

The greatest benefits of this meditation come with daily practice. One should therefore strive to set aside a daily time for it.

EXERCISE

Try *hisbodedus* for five minutes a day, at the same time and place. It is not necessary to ask and answer all of the questions, although you may find it useful to do so. At the end of each session (or even during), jot a few notes about your answers.

•

THE MEDIUM IS THE MESSAGE

The exercise of *hisbodedus* can lead to a deeper self-awareness. Still, as demonstrated at the beginning of this chapter, clear information about oneself is not very useful without an objective standard of goodness. We further defined the ultimate standard as the Infinite, unchanging source itself.

This standard of morality leaves a major hurdle to overcome.

For the philosophical framework of Chapter 2 posited that this something we are calling Infinite that created this universe is unknowable by finite beings such as ourselves. How, then, can it serve as a useful standard of goodness?

Recall the reason, as it were, that Judaism uses to explain the creation of this finite universe: the ultimate act of altruism, completely for the self-fulfillment of the creatures in the universe.

According to this philosophy, one might well wonder what kind of altruist gives someone a complicated and potentially dangerous machine without instructions.

In the 1988 film *Beetlejuice,* the protagonists find themselves in a world after death and they cannot make sense of what is going on around them until they find an instruction book. Until then, they stumble from mistake to mistake, having a miserable time. The maître d' of the afterworld scolds them for not reading the instruction book. If they had only opened their eyes they would have found the *Handbook for the Recently Deceased* on the coffee table.

> *This life is a test: this is only a test. Do not attempt to adjust*
> *your life. If this had been a real life, you would have*
> *been provided with instructions. . . .*
>
> ANONYMOUS

In fact, we have such an instruction book. It is called Torah. The word literally means guide or instructions. Some people think it means Bible or law but these are mistranslations. In modern Hebrew, driving instructions are called *torat hanhaga* and home economics is called *torat bayit.* The ancient name Torah is short for *Torat Chayim*—guidebook to life.[3] It is, someone once remarked, the original *Life's Little Instruction Book.*

Practically speaking, centuries of exile and persecution have dealt a heavy blow to Torah knowledge and we no longer know how to access its wisdom on every detail of life. Today, if you want to know how to make money, go to business school, and if you want to learn how to heal people, go to medical school. But if you want to know how to enjoy your money, how to pursue happiness, it is possible to find tremendous guidance in the Torah.

Key to Kavana

Prior to your 5-minute *hisbodedus* session, remind yourself: By introspecting and working on the "big questions," you are actualizing your spiritual potential. This prep brings you one step closer to fulfillment of your life's purpose.

As a guidebook, the Torah is relevant to anyone: Atheist, Conservative, Orthodox, Reconstructionist, Reform, and Secular. It also contains much wisdom relevant to non-Jews.[4] Like any guidebook, it can be used by each person differently but is utterly useless to one who does not examine it.

TRANSCENDENTAL GOODNESS

With or without the Torah, one continues to face moral choices every day. When confronting these daily dilemmas produced by the soul-body struggle, pause for a moment and recall that the Infinite source of existence must also be the source of this dilemma. In other words, the sister tempted to hit her brother should think: I was given this moral choice in order to make me a better person! *Wow!* What a wonderful gift!

Thus, each moral choice, from the most minute to the most grave, can become a moment of transcendental amazement as well. Every time I confront my own shortcomings and attempt to mend them, I can recall that this situation itself is a gift from the Infinite source of all, in order to make me a better person: a personalized transcendental gift. That idea is truly amazing to consider.

NOTES

1. With no sense of irony, UN Secretary-General Kofi Anan spoke thus of Israel during its military response to such violent assaults.
2. Kaplan, *Jewish Meditation,* p. 17.
3. Cf *Gur Aryeh* on Genesis 1:1.
4. *Torah* refers to both the written Torah (the "Bible") and the oral Torah, which includes the Talmud, Midrash, and Kabbalah.

EIGHT

•

CREATIVITY

The Art of Yourself

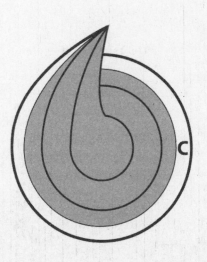

The Effort and Reward of Creativity

Transcendental Creativity

The Life Meditation

Karma

Internal Structure

Yin-Yang Theory

The Sea Change

The Ultimate Creativity

Solitary v. Group Power

A favorite saying of Rava: "The goal of wisdom is
returning to one's ideal state . . ."

TALMUD[1]

Perhaps the supreme act of creativity would be the creation of a world—a big bang, something from absolutely nothing. As far as we know, only an Infinite can do that.

Human beings are creative when we make something productive and useful from that which is inert. For example, we transform iron and other elements into a 747 that can transport people from one place to another. Or we spread a pallet of formless paint onto canvas to create a beautiful scene.

The ultimate creativity available to us is the creation and transformation of people. This creativity is qualitatively superior to self-transformation. After all, what rank would most people rather hold in the army, private or general?

Even though the army could not function without soldiers who play a vital and meaningful role in defending the country, there is a greater degree of satisfaction in the role of general, because that position allows greater creativity than simply following orders. The same rules apply to a business: higher levels of responsibility can be more pleasurable in their own right, regardless of the greater compensation.

THE EFFORT AND REWARD OF CREATIVITY

Recall the struggle required to achieve personal morality: overcoming the trap of public image, to do what is good rather than what looks good.

Similarly, the effort and real joy of social creativity is to conduct the orchestra for the music and not for the power trip. Any position of power can induce one to focus on controlling others rather than helping them.

Control is, of course, a factor in creativity—one must control the creative act to some degree (for instance, the artist must exert control over eye, arm, and brush in order to translate ideas into reality).

But people sometimes make the mistake of confusing the material pleasure of control with the spiritual pleasure of creativity. Stalin, Pol Pot, Saddam, and a long list of other tyrants went for control—i.e., power—but their pleasure was only material, illusory creativity. Spiritual (real) creativity requires the focus on helping others raise themselves.

The way to tell if you are being creative or simply controlling is by analyzing your intentions: how would you feel if someone else took over and completed the job? You can also look at the results: whereas spiritual creativity gives other people pleasure, control makes you feel powerful.[2]

Jewish tradition maintains that helping someone for whom we care is the greatest earthly pleasure we can have.[3] If so, then cultivating love and compassion for others must be a prerequisite to this creative pleasure.

EXERCISES

1. List five situations in which you are or were in a position of power over others, or in which someone else is or was in a position of power over you. Check those that were creative experiences and those that were controlling power trips.

2. What are the characteristics of an ideal leader?

TRANSCENDENTAL CREATIVITY

The transcendental dimension of creativity has two facets: appreciation and imitation.

Appreciation on this level is no different from previous areas discussed. While helping others the ultimate pleasure comes from being thankful for the ability and wherewithal to do so. The creative pleasure instantly becomes a transcendental experience too.

Now, since the ultimate creator is the Infinite, to be creative is to be most Infinite-like. A person who strives to help others is imitating the Infinite. Ergo, the greatest creative pleasure is found in the greatest altruism, and in this regard a person imitates the Infinite—the ultimate altruistic giver.

The hurdle that prevents many people from reaching their fullest creative potential is the steady corruption of the psyche by years of bodily, material experiences that cloud one's ability to tap into one's true inner nature. There are temporary meditative solutions that allow momentary clarity. However, to completely reprogram the psyche according to the ideal Infinite model requires a daily "surgical" meditation that can slice through the layers of ego and unveil the shining creative self within.

THE LIFE MEDITATION

The life meditation comes as a response to this need for a systematic way to reach our individual and collective potential.

Prior to and during the First Temple era, when classical Hebrew was still spoken and prophecy was as common as grapevines, there were many keys available to unlock the inner creative self.

After devastation and exile circa 350 B.C.E., the Judaic Supreme Assembly faced three problems: Jews were now scattered around the world, losing touch with each other; Hebrew was no longer a mother tongue; and the Jewish meditative arts were being forgotten.

This assembly included the leading Torah sages and mystics. These are the same mystics who composed most of the *brachos* presented in Chapter 5. In addition to the *brachos,* they created the mantra-like life meditation.

In contrast to ordinary, brief mantras that are personalized, the life meditation is an intricate "mantra" for all Jews to say every day. It is written in high Hebrew and thereby able to encapsulate some of the most esoteric concepts. Three of the seventy-two mystics of the Supreme Court were certified prophets, which means that the life meditation is also, to some extent, written in the language of prophecy.[4]

Because most people say the meditation standing, it earned the nickname, "the standing," or *Amida.*

External Structure

Recall the concept of the *bracha* as the archetypal transcendental moment. A single *bracha* elevates one narrowly defined experience to the transcendental realm.

The *Amida* is a series of eighteen *brachos*. In numerology (*gematria*), eighteen represents *chai,* the Hebrew word for life. Each *bracha* in the meditation operates within a specific area of consciousness and transcendence. Under deep analysis, their pattern also mirrors human history as well as an individual's life cycle. On the simplest level, this string of eighteen *brachos* is a tremendous key to unlocking human potential.[5]

In some ways, the *Amida* is the counterpart of the *Sh'ma.* Their contrasting qualities complement each other:

	Sh'ma *Meditation*	Amida *Life Meditation*
method	transcend this world	fully focus on this world
metaphor	go "up" to the Infinite	bring the Infinite "down"
result	nullify self	transform self
psychology	receive and give love	self-analysis

Whereas the *Sh'ma* opens the gates of pure love for us, the *Amida* is more like a full psychoanalysis.

In Hebrew, this meditation is sometimes called *hispalayl,* which literally means "examine oneself." This term reflects the concept that nothing we say will change the Infinite. By definition, the Infinite is unchanging (Chapter 2).

This unusual mantra is a complex meditation that, compared to the *Sh'ma,* takes tremendous time and self-discipline for success.

The Amida *as a Mantra*

How does the *Amida* compare to an ordinary Eastern mantra?

An Eastern mantra is a short phrase repeated over and over to train the mind toward certain thought patterns and away from others. Typically, a person will sit for thirty to sixty minutes saying a mantra hundreds of times until the words become the mind's sole focus. Having thus internalized the words, one continues to repeat them throughout the day in a continuous effort to control the mind.

The Jewish version of this type of mantra meditation is called *higayon* (see chart in Appendix D).

The *Amida* is somewhat different. Contrast:

	Simple Mantra (higayon)	*Amida* (hispalayl)
Length	Short phrase (2–10 words) conveying one main idea	Long series of phrases (650–700 words) which convey many complex nuances of one main idea
Times Per Session	Hundreds	1
Times Per Day	Thousands	1–4

The *Amida* is customarily repeated several times a day. In that sense it resembles a mantra. Those who make the effort to use it daily usually come to memorize it. They then can begin to see the meditation as an organic whole, repeated over and over throughout one's life, each time taking one to deeper and deeper levels of self-consciousness and higher and higher planes of transcendence.

It would be unrealistic to repeat this meditation much more often. It is too difficult. To say it once can take anywhere from five to twenty minutes, depending on one's personal rhythm. Moreover, to say it with proper *kavana* requires a warm-up and warm-down.

As a mantra, the *Amida* is a key to unlock the door to the inner self. Unlike the Eastern mantra, it does not serve primarily for mental discipline. The discipline of saying it daily results in an emotional, cathartic *cleansing*. Western culture offers catharsis mainly via theater and spectator sport; the Jewish seeker finds it within the self and in a daily struggle to become a greater human being.

Whereas the goal of the Eastern mantra is to learn *how to be* and Western prayer is for *having* something that I lack, the *Amida* meditation—indeed, all of Jewish spirituality, ultimately—is about *being* and *becoming*.[6]

This distinction explains the enigmatic form of the *Amida*. Rather than repeat a short phrase hundreds of times, we say a very long phrase only once at a time. While repetitive and vocalized like a simple mantra (*higayon*), the *Amida* is much longer and expresses complex ideas. Semantically, these ideas resemble supplicatory prayer, which is the stereotypical Western meditation. In other words, the *Amida* looks like a mantra that is expressed like a prayer or like a prayer that is said repetitively like a mantra.

The Amida *as a Prayer*

Western prayer has two defining elements:

1. *Petitioning* to receive something
2. *Pouring out* one's emotions

To whom are we petitioning? To the Infinite? Asking the Infinite to give something is philosophically difficult. Are we asking the unchanging Infinite to change to match our desires?

How, then, can we pray? Can we ask the Infinite for anything? To ask for something implies that I want the giver to change his current intentions. If he already plans to give me something, why bother to ask? And if he does not plan to give it to me, how will it help to ask? Again, the Infinite by definition is unchanging.

It would seem that, according to the Jewish concept of transcendence, our conventional notion of "prayer" makes no sense.

Instead, when we examine ourselves (*hispalayl*) in *Amida* meditation, we are attempting to change ourselves in order better to mirror the Infinite.[7]

As for the second element of prayer, pouring out one's emotions, the *Amida* can do just that. Saying the *Amida* well, with the right *kavanas,* can significantly increase *deveikus.* This closeness results from a combination of focused attention and increased calmness.[8]

An analogy: Imagine walking through a dark tunnel with a trail of small buttons on the ground. Each button, when stepped on, generates a small amount of electricity, which is then stored in a battery. Yet the buttons are so small that it takes concentration to step on each one. You can walk through the tunnel without stepping on any, or you may step on a few or even all. At the end of the tunnel, there is a lightbulb. The last button is the switch to release the electricity stored in the battery and illuminate the way. Depending on how well you walked the tunnel, you may have anywhere from no light to much light.

The parable describes how this Jewish mantra works. At the end of the *Amida,* the meditator is "plugged in" to the Infinite to the degree that s/he navigated the meditation with *kavana*. At that final moment, when the lightbulb goes on, so to speak, the meditator has a golden moment to use that light to look within him/herself.[9]

Please recall from Chapter 2 the Hebrew term for plugging-in: *deveikus*. This controlled *deveikus* experience teaches us experientially the transcendental meaning of being alive. When practiced regularly, one learns over time to connect just as deeply in other, more mundane settings, adding real "Life" (i.e., transcendental awareness) to one's life.[10] Just as the body is sustained by continuous breathing, the soul thrives via life meditation.[11]

The actual technique is described below.

KARMA

Jewish tradition is of the opinion that each soul enters this world with a mission, many of us to work out certain unresolved problems from our last birth (yes, Judaism has long had a central concept of reincarnation!).[12] The Sanskrit word *karma*, which refers to these challenges, has entered the English language. One's karma also includes new difficulties that arise during this lifetime.

Every challenge that we encounter in life is due to karma.[13] As we grow and work out the karma, certain challenges disappear. So, for instance, a theoretical person with no karma—a totally righteous tzaddik—would always get whatever s/he needs whenever s/he needs it. As one of my teachers put it, "When a tzaddik reaches into his pocket he always pulls out correct change."[14]

Therefore, all of life's ups and downs start to make sense. Challenges are opportunities work out my karma. If I succeed in letting go of whatever I was clinging to and generating that karma, the challenge goes away. In other words, I do not change the unchanging Infinite; I change myself and this new reality of my self "allows" the Infinite to treat me according to a different set of rules.

For example, imagine a person who lost her job and can't find another. Perhaps her karma to work out at that moment is her emotional attachment to employment. When she meditates, attaches her mind and heart to the Infinite, pours out her heart, and finally detaches herself from "needing" a job, she has now changed her karma. There is no longer any karmic need for her to be without work and she will now find work. It's a simplified example, but essentially true; the hard part is to take that real step of growth and it may take her days or weeks of meditation to succeed. But over time, with much practice, one should be able to succeed after just a few meditation sessions—and most people do.

In a nutshell, the *Amida* is a Jewish approach to "how to get your prayers answered."[15]

Now, most people are aware of a distinction between the person they are now and the person they have the potential to be. We constantly strive for this ideal, and usually fall short. Why do we fail? Usually because we lack clarity on the ideal itself. Most of us lack the wisdom to visualize a true ideal.

The master mantra is a road map to the ideal spiritual person.

THE IDEAL ME   THE REAL ME

TRYING TO MATCH THE IDEAL   THE IDEAL ACHIEVED, MOMENTARILY

INTERNAL STRUCTURE

Dissecting the *Amida* allows the seeker who has mastered the previous lessons in this handbook to begin using the meditation meaningfully. The discussion will cover only a fraction of what needs to be said about the mantra, and upon completion of this handbook, the seeker is advised to consult advanced works mentioned in the Bibliography.

The meditation is a string of eighteen *brachos*. These eighteen form three distinct groups: the first three, the middle twelve, and the last three. Approximately 1,900 years ago (500 years after the mantra was composed), the mystics of the time added a thirteenth *bracha* to the middle group. The number thirteen alludes to unity and love (Chapter 6).

The first group establishes our bearings within the transcendental field, the middle group develops the transcendence until a climax at the fifteenth *bracha,* and the final group of three *brachos* form the conclusion.

Unlike the *brachos* discussed in Chapter 5, each of these nineteen is an entire paragraph. Each paragraph ends with the familiar language "Baruch atah adonoy . . ." To understand the purpose and ideal *kavana* of each *bracha,* we need to study the entire paragraph—a larger task than the scope of this handbook. Jewish tradition recommends that beginners say the meditation in any language they understand; therefore, any seeker who finds the full Hebrew text overwhelming should feel completely at ease to begin a daily meditation with an English version.[16] The text is given at the end of this chapter.

At this point, it is instructive to look at the last *bracha* of the middle group, which is in some ways the climax of the entire mantra. The fifteen previous *brachos* all build toward it, and the final three *brachos* are all concluding echoes after it. This climactic *bracha*'s tagline reads:

> **Baruch atah ADONOY sho-may-ah tefila.**
> *You the Infinite are the source, open to human transcendence.*

In other words, at the highest moment of transcendence during Judaism's central meditation, the *kavana* is to internalize the amazing possibility and the actuality of transcendence itself. Complete knowledge of this fact—the fact that we can transcend, that we can connect to the Infinite—is synonymous with transcendence itself and is therefore the object of our meditation.

The full *Amida* can be an amazing, transformative experience. However, it is almost overwhelmingly long and complex. Begin, then, with the first *bracha* alone. Indeed, the first *bracha* contains the lion's share of the cosmic depth and power found in the entire meditation.[17] It may be a worthwhile long-term goal to learn the full meditation. But in the meantime, the first *bracha* will get a lot of mileage.

The First Bracha

The first *bracha* is akin to turning on the power. Its tag reads:

> **Baruch atah ADONOY magen Avraham.**
> *You the Infinite are the source, the shield (protection and badge) of Abraham.*

What does Abraham have to do with our meditation? If said with concentration, we kindle emotions based on what we know about the life and personality of Abraham.

We actually know much about the life of Abraham. Among other things, we know that he is considered the father of the three monotheistic religions, which account for a third of humanity, and may be a progenitor of eastern spirituality as well (see Chapter 1). Whatever fueled him may be something worth plugging into.

But we also know that Abraham's wife Sarah was equally important as a spiritual innovator. In fact, she was in some ways his spiritual superior.[18] Yet, the mantra mentions Abraham but not Sarah. This subtle issue needs some explanation.

YIN-YANG THEORY

It is a basic principle of classical Judaism that not only is there no inequality between men and women, but on an idealized spiritual plane, there is no difference between them. Ideally, a man and woman are a single soul (*neshama*) that was separated at some time past into two and whose mission it is to find each other and become one again. We learn this concept from the story of the Garden of Eden, when the first human, Adam, is split in half. In fact, according to Jewish tradition, before the split, Adam is a kind of hermaphrodite, a person with both male and female characteristics. After the split, Adam and Eve are differentiated by gender.[19]

Therefore, when a man and a woman have an ideal marriage, they again become one soul. This concept is not simply poetic. Their souls actually merge.

Yet, the fact that Man and Woman were once a single soul and can become a single soul again does not mean that they are identical. Nor do they have the same roles in life. Similarly, although Sarah the individual was a greater mystic than Abraham, that does not mean that their spiritual natures were similar.

Rather, men and women usually possess spiritually distinct natures that are generally stereotyped, to borrow from Eastern vocabulary, as the yin (feminine) and the yang (masculine). Each person whether female or male possesses some mixture of the two tendencies. According to Chinese yin-yang theory, the feminine yin is characterized by internality, darkness, peace, and the Earth; the male yang is characterized by externality, light, agitation, and the Heavens.

Many ancient cultures developed variations on this theme and many modern religious groups have expropriated these symbols for their own purposes. Traditionally, however, the familiar yin-yang symbol of blackness and whiteness in flux represents the basic theory of yin-yang ideal of these two forces in equal balance. This theory guides traditional Chinese medicine, kung fu, and other practices.

Some readers at this point reach a cognitive impasse. The idea that there are significant differences between men and women has been nearly drummed out of our consciousness. In stark contrast, however, Judaism maintains that the obvious physical differences between men and women do represent similar hormonal, psychological, and mental differences as well. This traditional view has been somewhat rehabilitated in recent years thanks to the success of John Gray's book, *Men Are from Mars, Women Are from Venus,* a work that is entirely consistent with Jewish tradition.[20]

The Jewish Model

The Jewish model of the female-male dynamic begins with the simple yin-yang concept of complementary energies. However, the full picture is more complex. The interaction of the two is the diametric opposite of their natures.

Thus, Woman and Man might be compared to a cup and water. The cup holds the water. The interaction of the cup to the water is described as the cup holding or containing the water. Therefore, in terms of their interaction, the cup is the external and the water the internal.

However, the cup itself is "internal-looking." The cup's essence is defined by what is inside. We may decorate the cup, but its real value qua cup is in what it can do on the inside, not how it appears on the outside.

The water is the exact opposite. When interacting with the cup, the water is surrounded and protected by the cup. But by itself, the water is only relevant in its externality. If we look at the internal nature of water, we see two abundant elements, hydrogen and oxygen. We don't value water for these elements. We value it as water; we want to know if it's frozen, liquid, or gas; hot or cold; pure or dirty, all externally observable features.

The cup and water resemble the Feminine and Masculine principles.

First, consider the interaction of the Feminine and Masculine. In the most intimate relationship between Woman and Man, the external, enveloping Feminine interacts with the internal, enveloped Masculine. We observe this interaction on the biological level and it is mirrored in Jewish custom: the bride at a traditional wedding walks around the groom and not vice versa. The man is like water: boundless, groundless, and shapeless until the woman gives him bounds, grounding, and shape; in lay terms, he is homeless until she gives him a home.

Similarly, when we describe how the Infinite interacts with the finite universe we use the symbolism of male energy entering female energy, so to speak. The Infinite actively "dwells in" the world, as it were.

However, like the cup and water, Feminine and Masculine natures in themselves are the opposite of their interactions: the female can only surround the male because of her essential internality. Conversely, the male seeks refuge in her internality because he is an essentially external being.

One finds greatest spiritual strength by tapping into one's essence; therefore, feminine spiritual strength largely comes from that which she keeps hidden and masculine strength from that which he reveals.

BALANCE OF ENERGY   INTERACTION

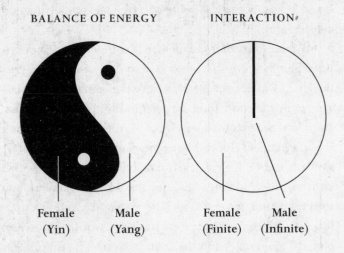

Female   Male   Female   Male
(Yin)   (Yang)   (Finite)   (Infinite)

Let us apply this model to the story of Adam and Eve. Adam begins with both male and female characteristics (Genesis 1:27). Gender appears when this hermaphroditic creature called Adam is split into two, male and female (2:21–22). Which of the two halves should we expect to retain the original name, Adam?

A name is an external representation of something. The half of this yin-yang duality that retains the external expression of their total spiritual essence is, by definition, male. Therefore, the original name for the total being—Adam—remains with the male half. The female aspect becomes his *aizer knegdo,* or "contrasting complement" (Genesis 2:20).

This story needs careful elaboration to avoid misunderstanding. To call Woman the "contrasting complement" (or "helpmate" in some translations) of Man is not a statement of contrasting value. On the contrary, her role is as essential as his in their self-actualization. Without her, he'll never amount to anything. Man's problem is that when alone, he is essentially unfulfilled potential. Man, qua man, is a creative idea, a blueprint; Woman takes his potential, his idea, his blueprint, and builds it into something real. That is her special power.

This differentiation is fully expressed in human reproduction, where the only thing that a man has to offer is a seed, a tiny drop so small that it's almost nothing, almost the smallest unit of information that he can produce. He gives that seed to a woman who then builds it into something he could never build—another human being. Without her, his ultimate creative potential is worthless. Together, when they become one, their creative potential is nearly boundless.

This model explains the roles portrayed in Genesis 18, where Abraham runs outside the tent and Sarah remains inside. Both are equally important in the story, but each represents an energy that complements the other. They are two sides of a coin, one visible and one hidden. We know that Sarah is part of the equation and it is no slight to her honor to be the keeper of the internal wisdom. But her mystical strength depends on her role as the hidden, internal side of the yin-yang, just as Abraham's strength depends on his role in the external world. Both halves are essential for a complete being.

Now it is possible to understand the focus in this mediation on Abraham, and, to a lesser extent, on Isaac and Jacob.

The *Amida* takes one into the very essence of transcendence.

That essence is expressed with a chain of ideas, as discussed above. The three forefathers—Abraham, Isaac, and Jacob—gave the Jewish people and the world specific potentialities that constitute our greatness as a people and as a species.

- Abraham: lovingkindness
- Isaac: pure transcendence
- Jacob: perfect harmony of heaven and earth

Yet where are the complementary wives—Sarah, Rebecca, Rachel, and Leah? Did they not also contribute to our spiritual potential?

The answer should now be clear. We do not mention the foremothers by name because, while each made a unique contribution, their spiritual essence is intertwined with their husbands. To name them in a transcendent, unifying meditation would be redundant.

Sadly, this spiritual differentiation has often been misused to take advantage of women economically and politically. It is no less unfortunate that generations have been educated to believe that women and men are essentially the same, when if fact we are complementary.

Sarah's dominant character trait is *din,* strict justice. Her primary spiritual mission is to shape Abraham's kindness. She is the one who initiated the banishment of Abraham's wayward son Ishmael; Abraham would never do so on his own. In fact, the Torah is unequivocal: "Whatever Sarah will say to you, heed her voice" (Genesis 21:12). Sarah is right. Abraham needs to absorb that measure of *din* from her.[21]

A similar pattern occurs with Isaac and Rebecca. Here, the tables are turned: Isaac, the quintessential transcendental man, is too severe with Jacob in Genesis 25:28. It takes Rebecca's special sensitivity and kindness to rescue Jacob in Genesis 27, instructing him to trick Isaac into giving him his due blessing. In hindsight, Jacob accepts this turn of events as correct in Genesis 28, when he ratifies the earlier blessing. Like Sarah, we see Rebecca's historical role completely entwined with and complementary to her husband.

As for Jacob and his two wives, Rebecca and Leah, the pattern shifts slightly. For Jacob has no fundamental lack: The Torah calls him *"ish tam,"* a perfect man.[22] Rather than complement him, his wives protect him from the outside world. They help Jacob disentangle the family from their malevolent father Laban, saying, "We have nothing more to do with him and we are with you." This statement of support demarcates a clear emotional and physical boundary around Jacob (and the Jewish people, whom Jacob represents).[23]

This model is the source of the Jewish custom, mentioned above, that a bride encircle her groom under the wedding canopy, symbolizing her spiritual protection of him. Because the pattern set by Jacob, Rachel, and Leah is our ideal model, Jews have always been called "children of Jacob" or "children of Israel" (Jacob's second name—see Chapter 2).

According to the radio analogy, with the first *bracha,*

we've switched on the power. Abraham (with Sarah) represents the transcendental connection in the most general way. Abraham's legacy is our collective ability to stretch to infinity, via most of the world's meditative traditions. Transcendence as we know it is an Abrahamic concept. It is Abraham's badge, as it were, or, in classical terms, his shield; hence, the first *bracha* of the meditation: *"magen Avraham"*— shield of Abraham.

LIFE MEDITATION—THE FIRST *BRACHA*

Baruch atah ADONOY elohaynu vaylohay avosaynu:
You the Infinite are the source, our power, and the power of our ancestors:

elohay Avraham,
The power of Abraham (lovingkindness balanced with justice),

elohay Yits-chak,
the power of Isaac (strict truth, balanced with compassion),

vaylohay Ya-akov;
and the power of Jacob (human excellence, harmony of heaven and earth);

ha-ayl ha-gadol, ha-geebor, v'hanohra, ayl el-yon,
*the power that is great (big), mighty (valiant), and awesome
(breathtaking), the highest power,*

ha-gomel chasadeem toveem u-konay ha-kol;
*the insurer of many acts of kindness and the invisible hand behind
everything;*

ha-zochayr chas-day avos
the fulfiller of the good karma of the forebears

umayvee go-ayl lee-v'nay b'nay-hem
and bringer of enlightenment to their children's children

l'ma'an sh'mo, b'ahava.
for the sake of its essence, with love.

Melech,
Director (the invisible hand, to the extent that we allow it),

ozayr,
helper (wherever we need help),

u'moshia,
resuscitator (giving us clarity of reality),

umagayn . . .
and shield (both in the sense of protection and as a spiritual badge)

Baruch atah ADONOY magen Avraham.

You the Infinite are the source, the shield (protection and badge)
of Abraham.

•

THE SEA CHANGE

When used well, the *Amida* causes a growth spurt every time.
In fact, there is a Hasidic tradition that someone who com-
pletes the *Amida* and is the same person hasn't said it with
kavana.[24]

The way to affect such a sea change, whether one says the
full mantra or only the first *bracha,* is to use the clarity it provides to access one's feelings. At the end of the recitation—
before leaving the meditative posture—let the heart start
talking. Express whatever it is that you have been feeling this
morning, today, this week, this month. The expression may
be, "I'm so lonely—help me overcome this loneliness," or "I
need to pass the exam, help me pass." The expression often
takes the form of a supplication because that form is particularly useful for bringing up the deepest emotions.

We do not need to think, however, that we are asking for
favors. Remember: the Infinite is everywhere all the time.
When we achieve a degree of *deveikus,* we are beyond passing
exams. That is not an issue. What is at stake is who we are as
people, our attachment to passing the exam. The result of

pouring out the little prayer at the end of the mantra should be that the sense of fear, urgency, or whatever it was that produced the prayer goes away, replaced by a stronger sense of amazing awareness.[25]

Techniques

The techniques for saying the *Amida* all enhance and accelerate its benefits.[26] The guiding principle should be to maximize our sense of awe, for awe (amazement) is what opens the doors of perception. As with the *Krias Sh'ma* meditation, one should strive to memorize the mantra. Memorization will occur almost effortlessly over the course of a few months for those who have the self-discipline to say it daily.

Position

The mantra can be said in any position, but it is best to stand with the feet together, knees slightly bent, and body slightly leaning forward. The mystics use an analogy of a king.[27] Imagine how you would stand in front of the most awesome king—say King Solomon or Julius Caesar or any monarch that you can imagine. That sense of awe is a fraction of what we should feel "standing before" the Infinite. The posture helps generate this emotional attitude.

The hands should be held close to the body, but not with the fingers clasped. This position mimics a *malach*. A *malach* is a spiritual entity that has no free will (because it has no material body). It is the agent of manifestation of Infinite energy into the Finite. Non-Jewish interpretations of the Torah have translated *malach* as "angel" and redesigned it with wings and a personality. We imitate the *malach* during this meditation as an additional tool to guide our *kavana* toward transcendence.

For greater *kavana,* the eyes should be closed, or, if open, gazing below eye level, to maintain the metaphor of standing before a king.

Location and Time

One should have a fixed time and place to say the mantra. Choose a time and place that will give you an undisturbed session every day. When you meditate at a fixed time you will find it very easy to increase your *kavana* and deepen the experience. The mystics who designed the mantra designated three ideal time periods for it: early in the morning, early in the afternoon,[28] and early in the evening.[29] They derived these time periods from the Temple service described in the Torah.[30]

The beginner would best start with any one of these time periods and to stick with it. In time, some decide to add another session.

If possible, the exact location should have minimal distractions. For instance, many prefer to stand facing a blank wall. Unplug the phone. Let your family members know that you are meditating and ask them not to disturb you during this time. After a short time, you and everyone else will grow accustomed to this meditation session as a part of the daily routine.

Warm-up and Warm-down

The mantra is mentally, emotionally, and even physically challenging. Like vigorous physical exercise, it should include a warm-up and warm-down. You are about to take a profound journey; don't dive in cold. Take a few minutes before you begin in order to think about what you are about to do.[31]

Many like to use specific songs of King David to stimulate the mind and emotions for the work they are about to perform. Each of David's songs (or psalms) is a "thought unit" that explores the details of a single emotion, similar in length and intention to modern popular music (while incomparable in poetic depth). Many find Psalm 145 particularly suitable for such a warm-up, which has been used as such since at least Talmudic times, and probably much longer.[32] The heart of the psalm is the verse

Ashkenazi/European:
Posayach es yah-deh-cha, umasbee-a
l'chal chai ratson

Sefardi/African and Middle Eastern:
Potayach et yah-deh-cha, umasbee-a
l'chal chai ratson

Open your hands and satisfy every creature of desire!

The need for a warm-down depends on how vigorously you exercised. If you just read through the mantra without great concentration, you probably will need very little warm-down. But even a moderate amount of *kavana* warrants another psalm and perhaps the Aleynu meditation, which, besides the *Sh'ma,* may be the oldest communal meditation in Judaism still used today.

Voice

If we truly felt appropriately amazed at the awesomeness of the Infinite, we would be speechless. Such awe is a high ideal—we should be so overcome with emotion that we cannot find the words.

Yet we are human. We are not so spiritual that we can successfully meditate in total silence. We need to utter words or else our minds will invariably wander. Therefore, the sages instituted a balance between the awe of the heart and the needs of the mind: to say the mantra in a whisper—so quiet that a person standing beside you could not hear you. Although whispered, this remains an internal meditation and the words ultimately turn inward.[33]

EXERCISES—THE LIFE MEDITATION (*AMIDA*)

Be in a quiet, undisturbed location. As with other meditations, it is preferable to say it in any language you understand if the Hebrew comes with difficulty.

1. *To begin:* This mantra gives multifaceted expression to the one-pointed unity of the *Sh'ma* meditation. Say the mantra in the morning, immediately at the conclusion of your *Sh'ma* meditation. Continue for four weeks.

2. *After this first month,* if you feel ready, add a second *Amida* session in the afternoon. (Some say that the afternoon meditation is the most powerful, and should even have precedence over the morning, if you only have time to say it once a day.)

   Say it slowly. The slower one says this mantra, the greater the potential benefit. Some suggest a pace of seven seconds per word, which brings the first paragraph to less than five minutes. If and when you get to the point of saying the full version of the *Amida,* you may complete the full meditation in five minutes (probably too fast) or in an hour (quite slow). The pace should be determined by one's ability to concentrate on the meaning of every word.

3. *At the conclusion of the second month:* Try to say the *Amida* in the evening. The mystics recommend a long-term goal of three regular meditation sessions every day. There is a very practical reason for this. We humans tend to be very this-worldly creatures, absorbed in our work, our relationships, and our recreation. For many, just making ends meet takes most of the day. This reality of our lives is the antithesis of transcendence.

Thus, in becoming transcendental beings, it helps to partition the day with meditation sessions: in the early morning before we get involved in the day's activities; in the afternoon, when we're most absorbed in activities; and in the evening, at the end of a day's work.

In this way, meditation becomes a tool to help us maintain an enhanced perception throughout the day.

•

THE ULTIMATE CREATIVITY

Recall the Jewish concept of the Infinite: an unchanging reality and the source of all pleasures in life. If one could tap into the Infinite itself, one could theoretically experience infinite pleasure. The meditative practices of previous chapters (awareness, saying *brachos* with proper *kavana* and so on) are effective tools to find great pleasure in life's minutiae, both their finite and transcendental qualities.

Key to Kavana

Prior to doing the *Life Meditation,*

contemplate the fact that the

Infinite is intimately involved

with every detail of your

life and the world.

Although satisfying, however, those meditations are incomplete. For as much as we were created to live life for the moment, we also have a duty to participate fully in human society and human history.

It appears that most people do sense this pull, even if subconsciously. Many of us strive to leave the world a better place than we found it.[34]

Paying attention to history and fixing the world are fundamental Jewish concepts mentioned repeatedly in the sources. Since Jewish spirituality should be a holistic path (see Introduction), this duty to history is expressed in the *Amida* meditation itself.

This long and rich arrangement of Hebrew words can connect us not merely to the Infinite qua Infinite, but to the infinity (small "i") as expressed in this temporal world, a world where we do perceive time and history. The *Amida* is a subtly poetic expression of the drama of history. While any *bracha* can open a connection to the universe in its *current* state, the *Amida* (with *kavana*) can connect us to the universe *as it is, was, and will be*—i.e., the way that the totality of the universe would appear from the Infinite's point of view, metaphorically speaking. That is transcendence.

William Faulkner wrote that "the past isn't dead; it isn't even past."[35] He meant that we, alive right now, are creating the past in our minds. Therefore, any talk of history should also talk of the human experience today. And that is indeed what we find in this master mantra, the *Amida*: it addresses both our immediate personal situation and our orientation to a collective history. It simultaneously works at these two levels.

SOLITARY V. GROUP POWER

Meditation is one of the most personal and private acts that a person can do. To develop a successful discipline, every tradition in the world recommends meditating at a fixed time and place, with few distractions—which may include other people (as per Chapter 6). These goals bring us back to a stereotypical image of meditation, with a lone guru sitting high on a mountaintop, meditating in complete tranquillity.

But Jewish tradition regards strict isolationists unfavorably. While temporary isolation can be an important means of introspection (as per Chapter 7), spirituality is supposed to be a part of everyday life, not apart from life. In fact, proper meditation teaches us an idealized model for life. For instance:

- While *brachos* are designed to help us focus and appreciate to capture the *wow!* of certain experiences, we strive to apply that same awareness and appreciation to every life experience—constant amazement.
- Once we begin to frame our day with a meditation on unity (the *Sh'ma*), we should strive for unity, harmony, and perfection in every action.

- Just as the *Amida* often works best in a group setting, so too we best face our most complex and challenging activities as a group effort, with the goal of helping each other make the journey (as opposed to competing with each other).[36]

On a practical level, the mystics who wrote the *Amida* actually recommended different dosages to men than to women. To men, they taught to meditate in a group. The strength of the group strengthens the individual. When we meditate regularly with a group, we are less likely to rush or to miss a session. The group also gives us the opportunity to compare techniques with other like-minded spirits. To women, whom the Torah considers in certain ways more naturally transcendent than men,[37] the mystics proffer no such specific advice, although today some women find group meditation highly beneficial.[38]

To balance these needs—the individual versus the group—Judaism has developed a combined strategy. On the one hand, we meditate when possible in a group. On the other hand, each individual's meditation is said in a quiet whisper as the mind gazes inward.

Unfortunately, it is not always easy to find a like-minded group. Very often, the individuals are sincere and dedicated, but they lack sufficient numbers to boost their individual efforts. So too, there are many groups who say the *Amida* in sufficient numbers but with poor *kavana* that can negatively affect the others. (I have attended group sessions where people actually start chatting when they finish their private meditation—even if others are still deep in meditation! This is an unfortunate situation that sometimes turns people off to Jewish spirituality altogether.)

The good news is that many Jewish communities already have one or more Jewish meditation groups who are really trying hard to help each other through a successful daily *Amida* session. Some of these groups are very small, pining for greater participation. Seek them out. You will gain from the collective power of the group and you will help strengthen the others.

Spirituality is a personal quest, yet Jewish spirituality has survived only via Jewish communities. Moreover, the commitment to group meditation helps keep a community together. It is an interdependent relationship and a doorway open to practitioners of all stripes.

NOTES

1. *Talmud Brachos* 17a. The exact text reads: *Tachlis chochma teshuva umaasim tovim.* The word *teshuva* is often mistranslated as *repentance.* It literally means *returning.* But returning to what? It cannot mean returning to good deeds because then Rava's statement would be redundant. It therefore must refer to a state of mind. Repentance—i.e., regret for one's past actions or current state of mind—may aid the process, but one may also do what is called *teshuva m'ahava*—to return to one's ideal self via a pure desire for transcendence.

2. For a cogent contrast between Jewish and modernist philosophies of creativity, see R. Joseph B. Soloveitchik., *Halachic Man.* Trans.

Lawrence Kaplan. (Philadelphia: Jewish Publication Society, 1991), pp. 99–137.

3. *NH* 2:11 (near end).

4. Zechariah, Nehemiah and Haggai.

5. See footnote 10, below.

6. Rabbi Nathan T. Cardoza, *Critique of Western Civilization.*

7. More precisely, the purpose of the lacking is specifically to produce this relationship of asking and giving (*NH* 2:4).

8. *Eitz Haim J,* p. 61.

9. *NH,* "Eitz Chaim," p. 61.

10. *Talmud Shabbos* 10a describes *tefila* as *"chayei sha'ah."*

11. R. Shimshon Pincus, *Sha'arim B'Tefila* (Afikim Negev, 2001), p. 17.

12. Cf Medieval commentary on the Zohar by R. Yitzchok Luria (the Ari), "Sha'ar HaGilgulim."

13. See Rashi's comment on Ecclesiastes 3:11.

14. A new soul may not have karmic issues, and would have to seek other reasons for its birth. However, according to the Arizal, there have been very few new souls born since the destruction of the Second Temple (70 C.E.).

15. Ralbag, quoted in Pliskin, *Consulting the Wise,* p. 75. See *NH* 3:2:4. Cf Katsof, *How to Get Your Prayers Answered.*

16. *Talmud Brachos* 40b; *Talmud Shavuos* 39a; *Talmud Sotah* 33a; cf *Magen Avraham* on *Shulchan Aruch Orach Chaim* 62:1.

17. *Gilu v'Ra'ada.* Cf Maimonides, *Hilchos Tefila* 10:1.

18. Cf Genesis 21:12.

19. *Talmud Brachos* 61a.

20. "Unlike its mathematical counterpart, ontological equality is not expressed in sameness or identity. While the Torah, assuredly, does not discriminate against men or women, undoubtedly it does discriminate between them" (R. Mayer Twersky, attributed).

21. Genesis 21:12.

22. Genesis 25:27.

23. Genesis 31:14–16.

24. Attributed to the Baal Shem Tov.

25. R. Shimshon Pincus, *loc. cit.*, pp. 26–55, p. 130, pp. 180–83.

26. Cf *Talmud Brachos* 31a.

27. *Talmud Brachos* 28b; *Orach Chayim* 98.

28. It is appropriate any time from thirty minutes after "true noon" (when the sun is straight overhead) until sunset.

29. If necessary, anytime at night.

30. Cf Numbers ch. 28; Psalms 145; *Talmud Brachos* 6b.

31. Cf R. Shimshon Pincus, *loc. cit.*, p. 20.

32. *Talmud Brachos* 4b.

33. Cf *R. Shimshon Pincus*, loc. cit., p. 133.

34. Jews participate in grass-roots social, political, intellectual, and religious movements in vastly disproportionate numbers, comprising anywhere from 20 to 50 percent of the participants in many political activities, New Age groups and academic revolutions. See Rodger Kamenetz, *The Jew in the Lotus*, p. 9. Some interpret this high Jewish participation as a more general Jewish drive to excel in any area of endeavor.

35. *Requiem for a Nun* (1950), p. 92.

36. Avraham Davis makes a similar point: "If we truly wish to make progress in our spiritual life, we must attach ourselves to community—even if we don't always like it! The power of the group, of the minyan, has the power to pull us forward. This is not to say that we should settle for just any community, but it is necessary to give ourselves over to a community during the time we are there." *Way of Flame*, p. 119. Mark Vernon summarizes the textual and historical basis for this principle (*History and Varieties*, Chapter 2).

37. This general view is derived from the specific case of Sarah (see footnote 20, above). Cf the Talmudic discussions of a woman's greater *binah* and lighter *daas*: *Talmud Nida* 45b, *Talmud Pesachim* 88b, *Talmud Shabbos* 33b, *Talmud Kiddushin* 80b.

38. Recall the above discussion of the yin-yang relationship between men and women. Men and women are not identical; rather, we are complementary.

•

VIRTUOSITY

The Art of Becoming

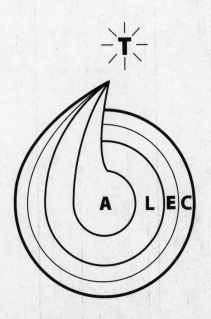

Pleasure v. Happiness

Why Judaism?

The Pleasure Virtuoso

*It is not in the heavens, that you should say,
"Who will go up for us to the heavens and take it to us?
and then we will hear it and do it."*

*And not across the sea, that you should say,
"Who will cross the sea for us and take it to us?
and then we will hear it and do it."*

*But the matter is very near to you,
in your mouth and in your heart to do it.*

DEUTERONOMY 30:12–14

The greatest expression of human creativity is to transform the part of the human that resembles the animal (the body) into a spiritual being that reflects the infinite spark within us, the soul.

We have a limited time—perhaps one or two lifetimes—

to accomplish this task. The basic path is to develop an expanded consciousness, which means to master both constant awareness and transcendent amazement.

This handbook has touched upon all of the prerequisite knowledge and many of the central details necessary to develop such a consciousness. As a course of study, however, it has left two important questions unresolved:

1. Why does it need to be so hard? Most of us are just dreaming of a day at the beach. Our entire culture is geared toward retirement. The thrust of the pleasure thesis contradicts the central values of the comfort-seeker.
2. Why Judaism—why should I choose this system, or any system? Maybe I will get more pleasure if I discover my own path.

In terms of effort, the art of amazement actually requires two efforts:

a. Learning *how* to enjoy the activity (becoming a connoisseur)
b. The effort of actually doing it (controlling the body's pull toward materialism)

The bottom line is that pleasure is hard work. This factor distinguishes pleasure from comfort, which, by definition, is a lack of work.

Consider the fact that some people go to the trouble of cultivating a taste for fine food, yet gulp down their meals. Some choose to lie on the beach their entire lives. Although entitled to choose their path, such people are trapped by the illusion that the body defines the self.

In fact, all materialist quagmires can be boiled down to a single mistaken belief, namely that pain and pleasure are opposites. It's easy to agree that life is for pleasure, so the conventional wisdom says: "Therefore, let us do all we can to avoid pain."

In fact, the absence of pain does not lead directly to pleasure, rather to comfort. All things being equal, comfort may be a desirable commodity, but it is not pleasure. It is merely the absence of pain or effort.

In fact, we need effort to get pleasure. Anything in life really worthwhile—good relationships, successful careers, the pursuit of meaning, and all of life's lasting pleasures—require a lot of effort to achieve. If we go after comfort, it is true that we will be rid of pain, but we'll also be robbed of almost any type of achievement. Without effort, there is no real pleasure.[1]

Rabbi Noah Weinberg uses a popular example of how pain and pleasure are related: He often asks people, "What are parents' greatest pleasure?"

Most people answer: "Their children."

"Where do parents find their greatest pain?"

Everybody gives the same answer: "Their children."

It is no accident that our greatest pleasure is also the

thing that takes the greatest amount of pain and effort. That is the nature of pleasure.

Every pleasure that we want in life has a price tag attached to it, namely the effort. The greater the pleasure, the greater the effort needed to acquire it. Superficial pleasures require far less effort in order to attain them. To truly appreciate each level of pleasure, we have to learn to focus on the pleasure and not on the price we are paying to get that pleasure. If we focus on the pleasure, we hardly notice the effort. But if we focus on the effort, we won't notice the pleasure.

Let's return to the example of basketball, from Chapter 4. Take a group of teenagers who love to play ball. On a good Sunday afternoon, they can play continuously for two or three hours. What would happen if we asked them to conduct the following experiment?

Play ball as you would normally, but we are going to take away the ball. We want you to run, jump, shoot, and defend against each other as you would if you were really playing.

How long could they play for? After five or ten minutes, they would start wondering, what is the point? Why are we being put through this exercise? They would say, "We've had enough of this! Please give the ball back." Give them back the ball, and they will play for another two hours.

Not only do we need a challenge—the basketball, a ten-foot hoop, a worthy opponent—but the amount of pleasure is directly proportional to the amount of challenge.

The mental effort of keeping one's eye on the ball—of focusing on the pleasure—is the essence of connoisseurship. In every category of pleasure, we have a choice: Either focus on the pleasure or focus on the effort. Focus on the effort, and we never want to get out of bed. Focus on the pleasure, and no amount of effort can deter us.

> *He who has a* why *to live can bear with almost any* how.
> NIETZSCHE

One of my memorable experiences in college was a seminar on wine tasting. We learned that wine is far more than fermented grape juice. There is a whole range of pleasures available in every glass. Wine has bouquet, color, and texture, and gives a different taste to different parts of the mouth. After learning to enjoy wine, we thought that only barbarians could guzzle a glass.

Life offers incredible opportunities for pleasure. A single

flower could give us hours of pleasure if we could sensitize ourselves to all of its exquisite details (Chapter 4). But without learning to appreciate such beauty, a flower gives a lift for a few minutes and then is forgotten.

For each type of pleasure, we have to learn *how* to appreciate the pleasure in order to access it. Just as wine is an acquired taste, every type of pleasure needs cultivation.

Yet cultivation is not enough. The soul may want to sip the wine, but the body is always there with its appetite, eager to guzzle.

The body will do anything to get its version of pleasure, just as an unbridled horse will roam freely. It needs to be reigned in and trained to go where the soul wants to go. When the soul properly guides the body, the body becomes a vessel for spirituality. Thus, the body becomes elevated.

This process of elevation occurs in minute steps, each of which is a free-will choice to follow the soul's inclination rather than that of the body. Such choices are where all the meaningful effort occurs. It is that very effort—which itself is minutely rarefying the body—that contains all of the pleasure.

The key to remember is that the desires of the body are not there to distract us or to be overcome. They are there to give us real, meaningful (and usually difficult) choices, for it is through the choices that we elevate ourselves.

As a rule, the body's materialistic pleasures are those experiences that require no mental effort and are basically physical-emotional experiences alone. This rule applies to every type of pleasure.

For instance, aesthetic pleasure requires focus and appreciation. Otherwise the experience is a form of gluttony.

Love requires focus on the beloved's goodness. Otherwise the relationship will vacillate according to variable physical and emotional conditions.

Goodness requires the effort of admitting mistakes. Otherwise, one will only be good when conditions allow.

Great creative expression requires focusing on others. Otherwise, one's creative energy will lead to as much taking as giving, and will depend on one's material and emotional state of being.

In all of these examples, the materialistic urge is more than a red herring: it allows the very choice that makes the experience pleasurable. The materialism provides the fuel to energize the spiritual experience.

Take the example of food once again. As much as one may become a gourmet, the pleasure of fine food is significantly diminished without an appetite. But with an appetite, one's entire being can resonate with joy at a fine, gourmet meal.

In the realm of love, physical desire can actually reach its fullest depth of expression in a caring relationship.

When faced with an ethical choice, it is only the impulse to be bad that makes the choice to be good at all meaningful.

Finally, in the area of creativity/altruism, the materialistic impulse to control can be the engine to run an enormous outpouring of altruism—as long as one makes the choice to focus on the needs of others rather than on oneself.

In all of these areas, it should be apparent, the actual pleasure is directly proportional to both cultivation (becoming a connoisseur) and effort.

This level of detail is necessary because pleasure is serious business! If someone came into a venture capitalist's office and said, "I have a great idea to help you make ten million dollars. Just invest a few hundred thousand dollars in me to get it going," the VC would not say, "Great. Let's go!" (not lately, anyhow). First the VC would investigate whether or not the deal is for real. This rule applies to any pleasure. We have to make sure that we invest our two most precious resources, time and energy, in pursuit of real, not counterfeit, pleasures.

Recall that this section on effort/pain began with the understanding that life is for pleasure, and that there are different types of pleasure to be had. It bears repeating that spiritual pleasure requires two efforts:

- Pleasure is proportional to cultivation, so become a connoisseur.
- Learn to spot the materialistic, counterfeit pleasures. They seduce us into not making the effort for true pleasure. They are the body's attempt to be in control and thus they enable us to make real, meaningful choices.

PLEASURE V. HAPPINESS

One of the most revered spiritual leaders, the Dalai Lama, is often quoted as saying, "I believe that the very purpose of life is to be happy." Superficially, it sounds as though Judaism and Tibetan Buddhism are saying the same thing. However, there is a distinction between happiness and pleasure.

Happiness refers to a particular state of being that one may or may not reach in this lifetime and in this world.

Pleasure refers to a process that leads toward happiness.

A simple example is a basketball game. The winners are typically happy, the losers unhappy. Yet, the pleasure is experienced entirely during the playing of the game. Pleasure is a process that does not depend on a specific outcome.

WHY JUDAISM?

What are the advantages to seeking pleasure through Torah or any system? Would it not be more pleasurable to invent a new system?

The answer is that not all spiritual actions are equally transcendental. Many indeed are completely illusory.

This point is easiest to grasp on the moral level. There are few in our society who would defend on grounds of moral relativism the act of flying an airplane into a building full of innocent people. Regardless of what the perpetrators believe, we do not believe that this action will produce even the modicum of transcendence. But why not? Why should that action be any different than feeding orphans? It is as if there is a filter that allows some actions to go through and others not.

Such a filter operates on every level:

Aesthetically, some sensual experiences are simply not conducive to transcendence. An extreme example is eating people. One may be a connoisseur of human flesh, but no amount of *brachos* with *kavana* will help us make that meal a transcendent one.

In the realm of love, most would agree that intimate love with a parent, sibling, or friend's spouse will not reach the transcendental plane.

We already mentioned morality, above. Terrorists are an extreme and easy example. It gets more difficult to identify the parameters of the filter when faced with issues such as: *What is stealing? When does life (and therefore murder) begin and end? Etc.*

An example of the filter concept in the area of creativity might be a case where one tries to help someone who does not want to be helped.

We clearly need a system to tell us which actions can make it across the filter to transcendence and which cannot.

Filtering is the primary function of the Torah. The Torah is a representation, encoded in story form, of this primordial filter between Infinite and Finite.

All that remains, then, is to study it.

THE PLEASURE VIRTUOSO

Imagine someone told you, "We have a little room back here. You can sit down and speak to the Infinite itself for a whole hour." For many people, would that not be the ultimate? The greatest pleasure, categorically above everything else, is to be one with the Infinite: to unite your own infinite spark with the source of all goodness and pleasure; to have such a keen awareness of the Infinite's presence that everything you do is accompanied by a sense of its love and guidance. That is the greatest pleasure.

To get it we have to pay a great price, to make an incredible effort.

The price is actually economical. It does not require growing your hair long or cutting it short. It does not require quitting your job or changing your lifestyle. The greatest pleasure is spiritual and has a spiritual price: *gratitude*. In order to connect to the Infinite with love, one must learn to appreciate all the good that it has done. That means giving up the illusion that we alone are responsible for everything we have achieved and admitting that everything we have is a gift from the Infinite.

This is a very difficult awareness to sustain because a human being's ego always craves recognition and independence; it balks at the concept of indebtedness to a "Higher Power." A person always prefers to believe that he has done everything himself.

If, however, one makes the effort to recognize and appreciate the uncountable wonders that the Infinite has given us, we learn to sense its presence in every aspect of our lives. We should be overwhelmed by the good that it has bestowed upon us and we should achieve a transcendence that begets a pleasure far and above any of the four categories below it. The greatest pleasure is the intensely rewarding experience of closeness to the Infinite. This experience is the ultimate goal for which humanity was created.

Focus on what you are living for. Work at it. You are here for pleasure, but it is good, hard work. It is hard work to be a champion Olympic runner, and even harder work to use all of our tools to become a champion human being. But that's the only way to get all the pleasures. You were not born to be comfortable. You were born to have pleasure—first class pleasure.

Just as we want only the best for our children, the Infinite Giver does not intend anything less for us.

Level	Pleasure	Counterfeit	Effort
1	Transcendence	Idolatry ("false gods")	Appreciation (Amazement)
2a	Creativity	Power/control	Taking responsibility
2b	Ethics	Looking good/ "success"	Accountability (admit mistakes)
3	Love	Infatuation	Commitment
4	Aesthetic	Gluttony	Self-discipline

This chart shows the hierarchy of pleasures, along with their counterfeit and the effort involved in getting the real thing.

However, the chart contains a serious conceptual flaw. For, although Infinite pleasure is indeed qualitatively higher than the others, since it is infinite, it is actually available via each of the other types. In other words, one can reach infinite pleasure via each of the levels, irrespective of the other levels. This immediacy is the basic characteristic of transcendence.

For instance, in order to enjoy food qua food—to enjoy the aesthetic experience of food—I need to slow down, notice the details, and savor. But if, in addition to that sensory enjoyment, I appreciate that this food comes from the Infinite source of everything and that it is a gift to me, then I can instantly transform the pleasure of eating into infinite pleasure. That appreciation is another word for amazement and is the incredible nature of infinite pleasure—it is readily accessible at all times.

Therefore, to capture this transcendental potential within every category of pleasure in the hierarchy, we have used the "wave" diagram:

The only problem with the wave is that it implies that any aesthetic, loving, ethical, or intellectual pleasure could also become transcendental, with the input of a little appreciation or amazement.

Yet we demonstrated above that there exists some kind of filter that allows some actions with *kavana* to truly transcend while others fail.

Therefore, a more representative diagram would show that filter as well as what is on the other side:

Thus, the letter aleph can represent this process. The scriptural aleph consists of two *yud* letters separated by a *vav*. *Vav* in Hebrew means *and*; it is always a link between two things. In this case, the *vav* represents a filter as well.

The *yud* below is pointing upward while the *yud* above points downward, for just as we strive toward transcendence, the Infinite seeks a relationship with us, as it were, for that is the purpose of creation.

The three letters that make up the aleph, namely two *yud*s and one *vav,* have the *gematria* (numerical value) of twenty-six, the same as that of the ineffable four-letter name.

The aleph itself has a *gematria* of one. This represents the ultimate message of the *Sh'ma* meditation. It also alludes to the true harmony of heaven and earth that humanity alone can create through harmonious thought, speech, and action.

Thought: can clarify ideas and seek truth
but: tends to wander and be lazy

Speech: used well, can focus the emotions
but: tends to be used carelessly, adversely
affecting the mind

Action: can focus and reinforce the thoughts
but: tends to be lazy and disconnected from mind

The realm of action will require a subsequent volume to elucidate. May the present volume be a useful piece of the grand puzzle that readers find before them.

NOTES

1. The relationship between pleasure and pain is central to Aristotle's *Ethics,* according to the interpretation of René Gauthier, where Aristotle maintains that one can only be *eudaimon* (happy) via a process that requires effort. See *L'Ethique à Nicomaque,* ed. and trans. René-Antoine Gauthier and Jean-Yves Jolif, 2nd ed., (Louvain: Publications Universitaires, 1970).

APPENDICES

Appendix A

Bibliography
of Works Cited and Further Readings

Abbreviations used in the endnotes:

MB—Mishna Berura (R. Yisroel Meir Kagan nineteenth–twentieth century)

MR—Midrash Raba (Talmudic sage Raba, second century)

MT—Mishna Torah (Maimonides, twelfth century)

NH—Nefesh HaChaim (R. Chaim Velozhin, eighteenth century)

SA—Shulchan Aruch (R. Joseph Caro et al., sixteenth century)

Talmud—Babylonian Talmud (fifth–sixth century)

Y—Jerusalem Talmud (fourth century)

JEWISH SOURCES CITED

Aaron, Rabbi David. *The Endless Light.* New York: Berkeley Trade Paperbacks, 1998.

Avudraham, R' David ben Yosef of Seville. *Sefer Avudraham* (circa 1450 liturgical commentary; various printings).

Bachya, Rabenu (Rabbi Bachya ben Joseph ibn Paqua), *Chovot ha-Levavot./ Duties of the Heart.* Trans. from the Arabic into Hebrew by R. Yehuda ibn Tibbon and into English by Moses Hyamson. New York: Feldheim, 1986 (2 volumes).

Bension, Ariel. *The Zohar in Moslem and Christian Spain.* New York: Hermon Press, 1932.

Cardozo, Rabbi Nathan Lopes. *A Critique of Western Civilization* (cassette recording). Jerusalem: Bar-On, 1995.

———. *Tefila* (cassette recording). Jerusalem: Bar-On, 1997.

Dessler, Rabbi Eliyahu E. *Strive For Truth (Michtav Me-Eliyahu).* Aryeh Carmell, trans. New York: Feldheim, 1978.

Forst, Rabbi Binyamin. *The Laws of B'rachos.* New York, Mesorah, 1990.

Glazerson, Matityahu. *From Hinduism Back to Judaism.* Jerusalem: Himelsein Glazerson, 1984.

Heschel, Abraham Joshua. *God in Search of Man: A Philosophy of Judaism.* New York: Farrar, Straus and Giroux, 1955.

———. *Moral Grandeur and Spiritual Audacity: Essays.* New York: Farrar, Straus and Giroux, 1996.

Hirsch, Rabbi Samson Rafael. "Commentary to the Torah," Isaac Levy, trans., in *The Pentateuch: Translated and Explained by Rabbi Samson Raphael Hirsch.* New York: Judaica Press, 2nd Ed.

Kahn, Rabbi Ari D. *Explorations.* Southfield, Mich.: Targum, 2001.

Kamenetz, Rodger. *The Jew in the Lotus.* New York: HarperCollins, 1994.

Kaplan, Rabbi Aryeh. *Jewish Meditation.* New York: Schocken, 1985.

————. *Meditation and the Bible.* York Beach, Maine: Samuel Weiser, 1978.

Kelemen, Rabbi Lawrence. *Permission to Believe: Four Rational Approaches to the Torah's Divine Origin.* Southfield, Mich.: Targum, 1996.

Kirzner, Yitchok. *The Art of Jewish Prayer.* Northvale, N.J.: Aronson, 1991.

Liadi, Rabbi Schneur Zalman. *Likutei Amarim Tanya* (Bilingual Edition). New York: Kehot, 1998.

Lunzano, Rabbi Menachem. *Derech Chayim.* A modern reprint of a section of *Sh'tay Yadose,* 1618.

Luria, Rabbi Yitzchok. *Kitvei Ari* (11 Vols.) Jerusalem: Vidvasky, 1988.

Luzatto, Rabbi Moshe Chayim. *Daas Tvunos/The Knowing Heart: The Philosophy of God's Oneness* (Shraga Silverstein, trans.). New York: Feldheim, 1982.

————. *Derech Hashem/The Way of God* (Aryeh Kaplan, trans.). New York: Feldheim, 1977.

————. *Mesilas Yesharim/Path of the Just* (Shraga Silverstein, trans.). New York: Feldheim, 1966.

Morinis, Alan. *Climbing Jacob's Ladder: One Man's Rediscovery of a Jewish Spiritual Tradition.* New York: Broadway, 2002.

Mozeson, Isaac E. *The Word: The Dictionary that Reveals the Hebrew Sources of English.* Northvale, N.J.: Jason Aronson, 1995.

Munk, Michael L. *The Wisdom in the Hebrew Alphabet: The Sacred Letters as a Guide to Jewish Deed and Thought.* New York: Mesorah, 1993.

Onkelos, *Targum Onkelos.* An authoritative, interpretive Aramaic translation of the Torah printed in most Hebrew editions alongside the Hebrew text. Also known as *Targum.* Circa 90 C.E.

Pincus, Rabbi Shimshon David. *Shaarim B'Tefila: Heraot v'Hasbarim al Asarat Sugei haTefila HaMuzcarim b'Chazal* (Hebrew). Ofakim Negev, Israel: Pinchus Family, 5761 (2000–2001).

Pliskin, Rabbi Zelig. *Consulting the Wise: Simulated Interviews with Great Torah Scholars of Previous Generations.* New York: Bnei Yakov, 1991.

Soloveitchik, Rabbi Joseph B. *Halachic Man.* Trans. Lawrence Kaplan. Philadelphia: Jewish Publication Society, 1991.

Tatz, Rabbi Dr. Akiva. *World Mask.* Southfield, Mich.: Targum Press, 1995.

Verman, Mark. *The Histories and Varieties of Jewish Meditation.* Northvale, N.J.: Jason Aronson, 1996.

Volozhin, Rabbi Chaim. *Nefesh HaHaim.* Wickliffe, Ohio: Ohel Desktop Publishing, 1997.

Witty, Rabbi Abraham B., and Rachel J. Witty. *Exploring Jewish Tradition: A Transliterated Guide to Everyday Practice and Observance.* New York: Doubleday, 2001.

OTHER WORKS CITED

Bacon, Francis. *The New Organon and Related Writings.* New York: Macmillan Library of Liberal Arts, 1960 (first published 1620).

Bamshad, Michael et al. 2001. "Genetic Evidence on the Origins of Indian Caste Populations." *Genome Research.* 11: 994–1004.

Bodian, Stephan. *Meditation For Dummies.* IDG Books Worldwide, 1999.

Boslough, John. *Stephen Hawking's Universe.* New York: Avon, 1999.

Crangle, Edward F. *The Origin and Development of Early Indian Contemplative Practices,* Volume 29 in the *Studies in Oriental Religions* series,. Walther Heissig and Hans-Joachim Klimkeit, eds. Wiesbaden: Harrassowitz Verlag, 1994.

Dass, Ram. *The Only Dance There Is.* Garden City, N.Y.: Anchor, 1973.

Ferris, Timothy. *Coming of Age in the Milky Way.* New York: William Morrow, 1988.

Fortescue, Michael. *West Greenlandic.* London: Croom Helm, 1984.

French, A. P. *Einstein: A Centenary Volume.* Cambridge, Mass.: Harvard University Press, 1979.

Gamow, George. *My World Line: An Informal Autobiography.* New York: Viking, 1970.

Goodman, Hananya, ed. *Between Jerusalem and Benares: Comparative Studies in Judaism and Hinduism.* Albany: SUNY Press, 1994.

Gribbin, John. *In Search of the Big Bang: Quantum Physics and Cosmology.* New York: Bantam, 1986.

Hadot, Pierre. *Philosophy as a Way of Life (Exercises spirituels et philosophie antique)*, trans. Michael Chase. Cambridge, Mass.: Blackwell, 1996.

Hawking, Stephen W. *A Brief History of Time: From the Big Bang to Black Holes.* New York: Bantam, 1988.

Holdrege, Barbara A. *Veda and Torah: Transcending the Textuality of Scripture.* Albany: SUNY Press, 1996.

Humphry, Derek. *Final Exit: The Practicalities of Self-Deliverance and Assisted Suicide for the Dying.* Junction City, Ore.: Norris Lane, 1997.

McNeil, William H. *Plagues and Peoples.* New York: Anchor, 1998.

Odenwald, Dr. Sten. *Archive of NASA IMAGE Space Science Questions and Answers,* http://image.gsfc. nasa.gov/poetry/ask/askmag.html

Olender, Maurice. *The Languages of Paradise: Race, Religion and Philology in the Nineteenth Century.* Cambridge, Mass.: Harvard University Press, 1992.

Poliakov, Leon. *The Aryan Myth: A History of Racist and Nationalistic Ideas in Europe.* Edmund Howard, trans. New York: Basic Books, 1974.

Rees, Martin. *Before the Beginning: Our Universe and Others.* Reading: Helix Books, 1997.

Rohl, David. *Pharaohs and Kings: A Biblical Quest.* New York: Three Rivers Press, 1997.

Shaffer, Jim, and Diane Lichtenstein. 1999. "Migration, Philology and South Asian Archaeology." In *Aryan and Non-Aryan in South Asia: Evidence, Interpretation and History.* Opera Minora, Harvard Oriental Series, vol. 3, ed. Johannes Bronkhurst and Madhav M. Deshpande. Cambridge, Mass.: Harvard University Press, 1999.

Yarris, Lynn. *Type Ia Supernovae Provide Direct Evidence for an Expanding Universe,* News Release, 1/7/99, Lawrence Berkeley National Laboratory, University of California (www.berkeley.edu/news/media/releases/99legacy/1-7-1999.html).

APPENDIX B

Online Teachers and Resources

Recommended Internet addresses for questions and guidance:

Contact the Author
seinfeld@jsli.info

Ask Moses (Chabad)
www.askmoses.com

Jews for Judaism
www.jewsforjudaism.org/phpBB2/index.php

Ohr Sameach Rabbinical Team
www.ohr.org.il/ask/

Project Genesis
www.torah.org/info/asktherabbi.html

Project Genesis public forum
www.torah.org/learning/torah-forum/

Rabbi Tovia Singer
www.outreachjudaism.org/questions.html

Worldwide network of rabbis from all backgrounds
www.jewish.com/askarabbi/All_The_Rabbis/

APPENDIX C

Major Types of Jewish Meditation*

Name	Meaning	Goal	Method
higayon/ hagig/ hagus/ haga	Mantra:	"State of pure existence": nullification of the ego	Vocal repetition of sounds, words, phrases, melodies. Often stage between levels of rina
hisbodedus	Isolation w. analytical introspection	Self-awareness	In daily isolation, ask oneself a set of penetrating questions
hisbonenus	Contemplation	Appreciation of relationship to the Infinite	Let the object guide the mind
hispalayl/ amida	Self-examining/ "standing" meditation	Realign one's will to the Infinite will	Daily repetition of a long "mantra" in deep concentration
ranan/rina	Explosive emotions that result in song	Bind to the Infinite with all emotions	Often used to prepare for haga, then return to rina at a higher level
shasha	Enraptured attention	Tranquillity	Contemplating Torah, with oscillating concentration

Name	Meaning	Goal	Method
Sh'ma	No translation	Internalize Infinite unity	Said morning and eve, to frame the day
siach	One-pointed introspection	Spiritual growth	Exploration of spiritual worlds
suach	One-pointed introspection	Full spiritual maturity	An ultimate consciousness via siach

*Based on R. Aryeh Kaplan, *Meditation and the Bible*.

APPENDIX D

Prophecy

PREREQUISITES:

Prophecy only occurs to a sage who is great in wisdom, mighty in deeds, and whom the material inclination does not control in any material thing; rather he continually fortifies his mind against his inclination and he is an exceedingly masterful intellect.

RABBI MOSES MAIMONIDES (1135–1204)[1]

DESCRIPTION OF THE EXPERIENCE:

There are many levels of prophecy. Just as one person may have greater intelligence than another, so one prophet can be greater in prophecy than another.

Yet all of them, rather than seeing a vision, they see their prophecy only in a dream or vision at night, or else during the day, while in a trance. . . .

All of them, while experiencing prophecy, the limbs tremble, the body becomes weak, and he loses control of his stream of consciousness. All that remains in his conscious mind is a clear understanding of what he is experiencing at the time. . . .

The information transmitted to a prophet in a prophetic vision is transmitted to him via allegory. The interpretation of the allegory, however, is immediately implanted in the prophet's mind, and he is aware of its meaning. Like the ladder that our father Jacob saw and the angels ascending and descending on it. . . .

MAIMONIDES[2]

HOW TO ACHIEVE PROPHECY:
The first step in prophecy is a strong desire. This is followed by meditation, which is its means. The goal is then the influx that comes to him.

RABBI ISAAC ABARBANEL (1437–1508)[3]

The prophets would meditate on the highest mysteries. . . . They would depict these things in their mind with their imaginative faculty, visualizing them as if they were actually in front of them.

When their soul became attached to the Supernal Soul, this vision would be increased and intensified. It would then be revealed automatically through a state where thought is utterly absent. . . .

RABBI MENACHEM RECANTI (1223–1290)[4]

THERE WERE VARIOUS METHODS:

One must learn these methods from a master. . . . They would . . . have to put themselves in a joyous mood. . . . They would then meditate according to their knowledge of the meditative methods. Through this, they would attain wondrous levels, divesting themselves of the physical, and making the mind overcome the body completely. The mind becomes so overpowering that the physical senses are abandoned and the prophet does not sense anything with them at all.

RABBI MOSES CORDEVERO (1522–1570)[5]

NOTES

1. *MT Hilkhos Yesodei HaTorah* 7:1
2. *Ibid,* 7:2-3.
3. *MT Hilkhos Yesodei HaTorah* 84:12.
4. Commentary on *I Samuel* 10:5.
5. Commentary on *VaYechi* (Lvov, 1880) p. 37d., quoted and translated in Kaplan, *loc. cit.,* p. 88.
6. *Shiur Komah* 16, quoted and translated in Kaplan, *loc. cit.,* p. 92.

APPENDIX E

The Seven-Minute Orange

This seven-minute version of Chapter 5 may be given to anyone—children or adults—who would enjoy improving their sense of amazement and their kavana. Try it with any sweet fruit in season.

INTRODUCTION

One of the main reasons that Jewish people do not get more into learning Torah is that it seems inherently impractical. . . . the Torah is full of interesting stories, but "It's not going to help me be successful at work or in my relationships, right?"

THE EXERCISE

So to illustrate just how practical the Torah can be, today I'm going to show you what it says about how to eat an orange. . . .

> [*Give each person: whole mandarin orange, one segment of
> a navel orange, knife, plate, napkin.*]

Now, each person should have a whole orange and single segment. To begin, please enjoy the single segment, right now, but do not eat the whole orange!

> [*Make sure they're eating, then continue.*]

The art of eating an orange, according to Judaism, is really the art of orange appreciation. . . .

Please hold up the whole orange and examine it. Notice its **texture**, how it looks and feels. Is it heavy or light?

[*Pause.*]

Smell it.

[*Pause.*]

How does it smell?

Have you ever noticed on an orange tree how these delightful globules stand out in contrast to the green leaves, just begging to be picked?

Please take your knife and cut the orange into quarters. Does the **smell** change?

Hold up one quarter. Imagine you were an alien from outer space and landed here on earth on a really hot day and you were quite thirsty, and someone said, "Have one of these."

[*Hold it up as if offering it to someone.*]

Would you know which part to bite into?

[*Usually they say no, in which case you continue.*]

Isn't the inside so much more juicy and inviting than the rind?

[*Pause for effect.*]

Smell it again.

[*Pause.*]

Now I have another question. What's this orange mostly made of?

[*Pause.*]

Obviously, it's water. Probably at least 90 percent water. But go like this. . . .

[*Flip your piece over so that the flesh is facing down and the rind is on top—wait for them all to copy you.*]

Why doesn't all of that liquid fall out? After all, we've cut it open!

[*Pause for effect.*]

[*Inspect the orange closely and say:*]

If you **examine** it closely, you'll notice that it is actually made of tiny little sacks that hold the juice. It's amazing!

Now, I'm going to ask a really practical, straightforward question. I'm looking for a practical, straightforward answer; don't get weird on me, okay? . . . How did so much water get into this form? In other words, if I were to give you a bucket of water, how could you transform it into some of these?

[*Hopefully, someone will figure out that you need to plant a seed and water it; if not, just remind them that this is how we make oranges.*]

But we don't generally water orange groves from buckets, do we? Even if we do, where does that water come from? Answer: The rain.

Where does the rain come from? Answer: Evaporation.

What causes evaporation? Answer: The sun.

Where does the sun get its energy? Answer: Left over from the big bang.

Now, when it comes to the big bang, science has to stop, because anything before that is unobservable and immeasurable. But according to Judaism, before the big bang, there was an Infinite God who created from nothing. What you have, therefore, is a direct chain of cause and effect from God to this orange in your hand! Are you starting to appreciate what an amazing gift this is? It's literally a gift!

One last question: we're all on a board together. Imagine that this were the Ford Foundation, and I walked in here today, held up one of these oranges slices, and said, "Ladies and gentlemen, I know what I want to fund next year. I want to fund the research to produce these things from scratch in the laboratory." How much are we going to have to invest to make it happen? Answer: Billions [or: Impossible].

Yet you can buy them for literally pennies! And today you're eating it for free! What did you do to deserve such a wonderful gift? Were you extra nice to someone today?

Now, to eat your second piece of orange, please close your eyes, think about all the wonderful qualities of this orange, where it ultimately comes from, how it is literally and figuratively a gift (and how you don't even deserve to be eating it, so to speak), and now bite into the orange, keep your eyes closed, and let it roll over your tongue, really taste it, and take your time before you swallow.

[Give them a long time—if you want, while they're eating, you can tell them a piece of orange trivia: In Florida, most of the oranges are grown for juicing, and in California, for eating, and they make jokes about each other's oranges. In Florida, they say that you could run over a California orange with a steamroller and not even get the pavement wet. In California, they say that if you want to eat a Florida orange you have to sit in the bathtub.]

How did the second bite compare?

[Ask for a show of hands for who enjoyed the second eating more than the first.]

Judaism teaches that—yes, your mother was right, slow down and chew your food—every bite of food we eat every day, everything else in this world, we should experience with that kind of intense focus and appreciation.

What about when we have difficulties in life, trials and tribulations? Any thoughts?

[*Chances are, no one will get it, but someone may.*]

Anyone here ever see Michael Jordan play, live or on TV? [Pause.] Who would Michael Jordan rather play 1-on-1— Magic Johnson or . . .

[*Dramatic pause with a mock-pride smile.*]

[*Say your name and point to yourself with mock smugness.*]

Why would he obviously want to play Magic? Won't he beat me so much easier?

It's obvious, isn't it? Pleasure in life is not the absence of pain! We find pleasure only through challenges, or "pain" as it were. No pain, no gain.

CONCLUSION

There is a lot more to say on this subject, but we're over time. If you would like to go into this topic in depth, please ask me later and I'll refer you to a certain book. . . .

But to conclude, does anyone know what the word *Torah* means? Hint: it doesn't mean "Bible"!

A: It means "instructions."

. . . in modern Hebrew, for instance, *torat nahaga* means "driving instructions"; *torat bayit* means "home economics"—what kind of instructions is the Torah?

[*Someone will guess—"for life."*]

That's right—*Torat Chaim,* instructions for living. Our challenge is both to bring the mystical into our life and to maintain the life in our mystical tradition, for this ancient wisdom called "Torah" underlies much of humankind's spirituality and ethics, and all of humanity can benefit from it.

Note to teacher—I don't believe it necessary to quote directly from the Torah—appreciating life in spite of the challenges is a major theme of many chapters in the Torah. For beginners it can suffice to preface the "Seven-Minute Orange" with a comment that the purpose of Jewish mystical tradition is to help us get the most out of life.

APPENDIX F

More Meditations

The following list of *brachos* is part of the traditional warm-up to the morning *Sh'ma.* They are listed here according to the customary order. Each *bracha* begins:

"Baruch atah Adonoy eloheinu melech ha-olam . . ."
You are the source—the Infinite (beyond all space and time)—our power, the director of the concealment . . .

Amazement

Bracha

**That I can relieve
myself at will**

. . . asher yatsar es
ha-adam b'chochma uvaro
vo n'kavim n'kavim
chaluleem kaluleem. Galui
v'yadua lifnay keesay
k'vodecha sh'eem yifasayach
echad m'hem oh yisasaym
echad m'hem, ee-efshar
l'heeskayaym v'la'amode
l'fanehcha. Baruch atah
Adonoy, rofay chol basar
umaflee la'asohs.
(. . . that made the human
being wisely and created
within one many holes
and cavities. It is revealed
and known on the
highest realms that if just
one were opened or just one
were topped up it would be
impossible to continue and
to stand before you. You, the
Infinite, are the source,
healing all flesh and doing
amazing things.)

That I have consciousness	. . . ha-nosayn l'sech-vee vee-na, l'hav-cheen bayn yohm u'l'vayn ly-la. (. . . giving under-standing to the rooster to distinguish between day and night.)
That I have eyes to see	. . . po-kayach eevreem. (. . . giving sight to the blind.)
That I have clothes	. . . malbeesh a'rumeem. (. . . clothes the naked.)
That I can move freely	. . . mateer asureem. (. . . releases the bound.)
That I can stand upright	. . . zokayf k'fu-feem. (. . . straightens the bent.)
That I have firm ground on which to walk	. . . roka ha-arets al ha-my-eem. (. . . spreads the land over the water.)

That I have shoes	. . . sheh-asah lee kol tsar-chee. (. . . that took care of all my needs.)
That I can walk	. . . ha-maycheen mitsaday gaver. (. . . strengthens a person's footsteps.)
That I'm a Yisroel with inner dignity	. . . o-zayr Yisro-ayl big'vuroh. (. . . empowers the spiritual seeker.)
That I have transcendental awareness	. . . otayr Yisroel b'see-farah. (. . . crowns Yis-roel with splendor.)

APPRECIATIONS

To the best of my knowledge, this book contains no original Torah; the ideas herein were learned from others. In addition to the textual sources cited, some of these individuals include: R. Yitzhak Berkowitz, *Shlita;* R. Dr. Nathan Lopes Cardozo, *Shlita;* R. Chaim Gogek, *Shlita;* R. Yosef Yitzhak Lerner, *Shlita;* R. Chaim Uri Freund, *Shlita;* R. Moshe Heineman, *Shlita*; R. Moshe Shapiro, *Shlita;* R. Mordecai Sheinberger, *Shlita;* R. Dr. Akiva Tatz, *Shlita;* R. Noah Weinberg, *Shlita;* R. Noson Weisz, *Shlita.* To list all secondary influences, namely the rabbis who taught me to learn and to love learning, would run this book over its page limit. The author accepts full responsibility for errors.

Others who have aided and abetted the process of producing this book include numerous manuscript readers and cheerleaders, including: Dr. Jeff Asher, Dr. Ina Bendis, Marc Beniof, Steve Blank, Brian Boyd, Raffi Cohen, Linella Devlin, Rabbi Yitzchok Feldman, Lawrence Gallant, Dr. Maud Gleason, Nat Goldhaber, Dr. Matthew Greenwood, Leah Kaess, Andrew Kaplan, Gutman Locks, Rabbi David Ordan, Dennis and Karen Seinfeld, Harmon and Jorun Shragge, Shoshana Wolf, and Patricia Wright. Thank you for your significant, *amazing* critical feedback and unending encouragement. Thanks to Suzanne Felson for inspiring the creation of Appendix E and to Alex Frankel for crucial technical support.

Thank you Neill and Linda Brownstein for your friendship and for helping bring the book and seminar to a wide audience.

Those who deserve acknowledgment but whom I have inadvertently neglected to mention, you are certainly appreciated.

No author in his or her right mind would neglect to thank his family. My parents taught me from a very young age to cultivate the present moment and to love all kinds of learning. My wife has been my complete partner in this labor of love. And our children will hopefully forgive me the creative pleasure at their expense.

Of all books, this volume ought to recognize with amazement the transcendental Source of all wisdom. During the creative process, it is natural for the artist to take credit. It takes effort to appreciate where appreciation is due.

ABOUT THE AUTHOR

Rabbi Alexander Seinfeld is a native of the Pacific Northwest. His interest in transcendental spiritual philosophy germinated while he was a student at Stanford. However, he credits his specific interest in the Jewish path to two years as a schoolteacher in rural Mississippi, surrounded by folks "who knew my people's book better than I did." This sense of illiteracy brought him to Israel to study. Seven years in Jerusalem yeshivas culminated in rabbinical ordination from Rabbi Zalman Nehemia Goldberg, *Shlita*. Based in Baltimore with his wife and children, Rabbi Seinfeld teaches around the world, both live and via conference call. He welcomes questions and comments at seinfeld@jsli.info.